Queen of the Turtle Derby

and Other Southern Phenomena

"I had some crab dip that Julia Reed made once that I would have eaten all of in one sitting, if I had been sitting, and if the other party guests hadn't dragged me off of it. This book is that good."

—ROY BLOUNT, JR.,
author of *Crackers* and *Robert E. Lee*

"Julia Reed's affectionate and hilarious observations about the Deep South and Southerners past and present are a delight to read."

—FANNIE FLAGG

"Not since Eudora Welty has anybody captured in such sophisticated, often mordant prose the brave, gracious, perverse, reckless, God-fearing Southern soul like Julia Reed does. Whether she's holding forth on fried chicken and catfish, guns, booze, cockfights, pestilence, or Southern womanhood, Reed loads both barrels and never misses the target. As a Carolina Tarheel, I rejoiced, cringed, marveled, and laughed myself sick at Reed's outrageous tales and savvy insights, and I defy anybody—Southerner and Yankee alike—to come up for air after reading the first chapter."

—JAMES VILLAS,
author of *Between Bites* and *My Mother's Southern Kitchen*

"This is a wise and tender book. Julia Reed is a loving defender of the South. Long may she live and write. She understands the deep seriousness that underlies our Scotch-Irish, English, and African roots."

—ELLEN GILCHRIST,
author of *I, Rhoda Manning, Go Hunting with My Daddy: And Other Stories*

"[An] effervescent collection of essays . . . charming . . . amusing."
                                        —*The New York Times Book Review*

"Ms. Reed writes about Southern food, fashion, women, and crime with enormous wit and charm and a vigilant eye for detail."
                                        —*The Wall Street Journal*

"These essays, each as refreshing and bracing as a mint julep, are full of unforgettable true-life cartoons. . . . Reed gives us a complex portrait of a contemporary South that's as full of grace . . . as of guns."
                                        —*Vogue*

"Reed, bless her heart, has written a laugh-aloud collection."
                                        —*Library Journal*

"Reed [writes] with wry humor and an agreeable appreciation of the absurd. . . . She deftly mixes personal reminiscences with facts and local lore."
                                        —*Kirkus Reviews*

"Reed celebrates . . . the Southern joys of fine dining and drinking, fashion and fun, and devotion to the spirit of Scarlett O'Hara . . . with fierce Southern chauvinism enlivened by wit and sophistication. . . . Entertaining others is a high art, too, and Reed can queen it over anybody in that department."
                                        —New Orleans *Times-Picayune*

Queen of the Turtle Derby

and

Other Southern Phenomena

JULIA REED

Random House Trade Paperbacks · New York

2005 Random House Trade Paperback Edition

Copyright © 2004, 2005 by Julia Reed
Reading group guide copyright © 2005 by Random House, Inc.

Published in the United States by Random House Trade Paperbacks,
an imprint of The Random House Publishing Group,
a division of Random House, Inc., New York.

RANDOM HOUSE TRADE PAPERBACKS and colophon are trademarks
of Random House, Inc.

Originally published in hardcover in the United States by Random House,
an imprint of The Random House Publishing Group, a division
of Random House, Inc., in 2004 in slightly different form.

"Trigger Happiness," "Southern Fashion Explained," and "A Plague on Our
Houses" were first published in *The Oxford American*, as was part of "The
Real First Lady." "Mysterious Ways," "Eat Here," "Lady Killers," "Tough Love,"
"License to Kill," and "That's Entertainment!" were first published in *The
Oxford American* under different titles. "American Beauty" was originally
published in *Vogue* in a different form. "Bird Song," "Member of the Club,"
and "The Morning After" first appeared in *The New York Times Magazine*.
"Cat Fight," Country Comfort," and "Queen for a Day" also appeared in *The
New York Times Magazine*, but in a somewhat different form and, in some
cases, under a different title. Part of "To Live and Die in Dixie" was first
published in *The Spectator*. "Whiskey Weather," in a slightly different form,
was first published in *The Independent on Sunday*. "Miss Scarlett" originally
appeared in *The Book*, a Neiman-Marcus publication, under a different title.

LIBRARY OF CONGRESS CATALOGING-IN-PUBLICATION DATA
Reed, Julia.
Queen of the Turtle Derby and other southern phenomena / Julia Reed.
p. cm.
ISBN 0-8129-7361-5
1. Southern States—Civilization. 2. Southern States—Social life and
customs. 3. Southern States—Humor. I. Title.
F209.5.R44 2004
306'.0975—dc22 2003058623

Printed in the United States of America

Random House website address: www.atrandom.com

4 6 8 9 7 5

Book design by Casey Hampton

To Jason Epstein

I hate to read. I don't get anything out of it. I never could stand to read. It bores me.

—Susan Akin, Miss Mississippi and Miss America, 1986

Acknowledgments

A friend of mine once gave me a cap reading AMERICAN BY BIRTH, SOUTHERN BY THE GRACE OF GOD. I share that sentiment in large part due to the Southerners I have had the good fortune to know and love, a list far too long for this space. So I shall try to limit my thanks to those who made my bicoastal (East Coast/Gulf Coast) life possible and who encouraged my endeavors on the Gulf end.

Philip Carter helped facilitate my move to New Orleans in the first place and served as a frequent source of inspiration. Elizabeth McGee Cordes and the late Michael Cordes provided sustenance, safe harbor, and countless nights of warmth and hilarity. Anne McGee looms large in several of these pieces, and, thank goodness, in my life. I am grateful to Ralph McGee, Benjamin Humphreys McGee, Jr., and Leon

Dixon, for illuminating many important matters; to Peter Patout, for his stout-hearted companionship and for sharing with me his Louisiana; to Anne Flaherty Heekin, for her steady stream of excellent clippings and observations; and to Jessica Brent and Helen Bransford, for pretty much everything.

Susan Nadler, the brilliant and unlikely Queen of the Peckerwood Nation, provided access to many of the greats of country music, as did her partner, Evelyn Shriver. Benjamin Humphreys McGee III did such yeoman's work researching the material for "Lady Killers" that he really should be listed as coauthor. Egan Seward made elegant order out of the chaos on my office floor and, as much as she could, in my life. Anna Wintour's loyal and patient support was invaluable. Mary Bahr's enthusiasm and hard work on this project finally shaped it into being.

Michael Boodro and Jon Meacham serve as the endlessly generous and talented shadow editors of practically everything I write, in spite of the fact that they have plenty to do otherwise.

I have dedicated this book to Jason Epstein, who has brought so many fine things into my life, and whose wise counsel and stubborn faith in me have been an immeasurable gift. I also want to thank my extraordinary parents, Clarke and Judy Reed, who have blessed me with their love and so much more, and my husband, John Pearce, whom I married in the middle of putting together this collection. The depth and breadth of his support—in all things—still astonish me.

Contents

Contents

Introduction

When I came back to live part-time in the South in 1991, I'd been gone for almost twelve years. I was born and raised in the Mississippi Delta, in Greenville, but unlike my fellow Mississippian Willie Morris, I had not gone "North Toward Home," I had gone north toward school and work, I had gone north to see the world (i.e., Washington and New York). It was a useful exercise—I did get educated (more or less), and I managed to find employment. I also realized that for me, the South was home, and I wanted—needed—to get back to it.

Of course, exactly what the definition of "it" is has long been open to debate. The South invites—in fact, almost demands—caricature, and two prevailing ones persist in these first years of the twenty-first century. One is that we remain hopelessly trapped in the past and have never quite managed to move beyond Jim Crow; we don't wear sheets anymore but we would if we could, and we still worship the Confederate battle flag. In this view, we are, at heart, gun-toting, beer-swilling, Baptist-church-going, pickup-truck-driving, Republican-voting good ole boys and girls with names like Billy Earl and Rayette. You might call this the "Scratchin' and Spittin' " school, whether they're tattooed rednecks or button-downed professionals. The other theory is that the South isn't the Cotton Belt anymore; it's the Sunbelt, a land of interchangeable suburbs, full of Home Depots and Blockbusters and people wearing Dockers pants. The old moonlight-and-magnolias South has been subsumed by the gods of commerce and big parking lots, and the only distinctive thing about the place, really, is that the accents are more pronounced in an office park outside Savannah than they are in an office park in Seattle. This is the "SUV and Soccer Mom" school.

The truth, as I hope this collection of my dispatches from the Southern front shows, is much more complicated and more interesting than either caricature indicates. The closer you get to the South today, the more you realize that America's most influential region—as the South goes in presidential elections, so goes the nation—is a tangle of passions and pastimes and habits of heart and mind that eludes any glib description. The South isn't the only unique part of the country (only the most self-absorbed Southern snob could think so in a nation that includes, say, Brooklyn or California). But it is my unique part of the country, and I believe understanding the South and its quirkiness, violence, and grace helps us understand America, too, in all *its* quirkiness, violence, and grace. And in any case, it's funny as hell: As reporters used to say of Richard Nixon, it never disappoints.

When I returned, it was, ostensibly, to write about Edwin Edwards, who, at sixty-eight, was running for his fourth term as governor of Louisiana. It was both a comeback and a last hurrah for Edwards, an astoundingly quick-witted politician also known for his gambling (he routinely checked into Caesars Palace under the aliases T. Wong and Muff Aletta, the latter after the delicious New Orleans sandwich of the same name), his womanizing (he once said the only way he could get in trouble with Louisiana voters was to be found in bed with a dead girl or a live boy), and his scrapes with the law (he was tried twice on charges that he'd sold state hospital contracts, but the first trial ended in a mistrial and in the second he was acquitted). I knew it would be an entertaining race, and when Edwards ended up in a runoff with former Klansman David Duke, it also proved to be remarkably tantalizing to my colleagues in the national press—not least because Duke neatly—hideously—reinforced the view that nothing much had changed down here in the bad old Deep South.

While I didn't have much fun with the creepy Duke, who, among other things, was just not very bright, I had a grand time traveling with Edwards. I became the sort of girl-mascot of the campaign, flying around in his small plane with only two advisers (cronies, really), touching down in Opelousas and Lafayette, listening to him preach to Pentecostals in Alexandria and oystermen on Bayou LaFourche. The men used cell phones, which were, in those days, very exotic and expensive, to place bets with their bookies on college football; they spoke in Cajun French when they didn't want me to know what was going on. Once, during a parade at the Shrimp and Petroleum Festival in Morgan City, Edwards greeted the crowds from the back of a pickup truck, blowing kisses and saying, "Hey, *chere*" one minute and cussing a blue streak under his breath the next as a trusty aide crouched down beside him calling out football scores that were, apparently, not such good news.

Edwards's disdain for Duke was, more than anything else, a class thing. In Morgan City, he was appalled at the sight of an otherwise skinny pregnant woman lining the parade route with a Duke sticker plastered across her stomach. At the taping of NBC's *Meet the Press* in New Orleans, he spotted Duke munching on a Baby Ruth and drinking a Coke—for breakfast—and he couldn't get over it. "That says it all," he told me at least a dozen times that day. Edwards had grown up picking cotton and for a while was a child evangelist, but he had put himself through law school and made it to Congress as well as the statehouse. He dined well (Ruth's Chris Steakhouse) and lived well (gated subdivision) and was so obsessed with cleanliness he washed his hands at least a dozen times a day. He had, in other words, made good; Duke was a pathetic loser not worthy of his attention.

He knew, too, that Duke would be a literal loser—record numbers of black voters turned out, as did the so-called enlightened gentry who ordinarily despised Edwards but knew they had no choice ("Vote for the Crook, It's Important"). Also, not even the most die-hard racist wanted to see every last tourist dollar leave the state. (The press was not nearly so convinced—it was Duke who had been booked to appear on the *Today* show the morning after the election. When Edwards found out, he refused to go on.) Edwards won by the second-biggest landslide in Louisiana history (he had already won by the biggest eight years earlier), and took up residence in the governor's mansion with his girlfriend (now his wife), Candy Picou, a nurse thirty-seven years his junior.

When the race was over, I found it almost impossible to leave New Orleans, where I still reside most of the time, so I stuck around. Duke almost immediately lost his overhyped political base and eked out a living by hawking his autobiography, *My Awakening*, and making speeches to Nazi holdouts in Germany and Russia. As it turns out, he also swindled his remaining supporters and failed to pay his income taxes, so in 2003 he began serving a fifteen-month sentence at the federal corrections institution in Big Springs, Arkansas. (The white supremacists next door in Mississippi got into even worse trouble. Former Imperial Wizard Sam Bowers was sent to jail, finally, for the 1966 murder of civil rights activist Vernon Dahmer, and Byron de la Beckwith was convicted, on the third try, of the 1963 murder of Medgar Evers.) Edwards, alas, didn't fare much better. In 2000, the feds finally got him on charges of extorting money from companies that applied for riverboat casino licenses, which they delivered to him in garbage bags full of hundred-dollar bills, passing them from car window to car window under the overpasses of Baton Rouge. He and Candy are still married, though Edwin, sadly, lives at the Federal Medical Center in Fort Worth, Texas, where he is serving a ten-year sentence, while Candy still lives in Baton Rouge.

The public demise of both Edwards and Duke became fodder for the second, Sunbelt view of the South. If two distinctively Southern species of politicians—the scoundrel and the racist—were now on the endangered list, if not completely extinct, it was proof, certainly, that the South itself was experiencing a demise of sorts—that it was becoming as bland as everywhere else. In the decade-plus during which I'd been gone, a lot had already happened to encourage this view, from the rise of cable television and global communication to the decline of the agricultural economy. The textile mills of Georgia shut down and they started making cars in Tennessee. John Edgerton wrote *The Americanization of the South*, and even Walker Percy worried that our suburbs—like suburbs everywhere, with their ennui and their strip malls—would be the death of us.

But when I returned I found everything still firmly intact. And I don't think that the fact that we elect slightly more responsible politicians and convict racists (at least the murderous ones) is going to change that. For one thing, the politicians are still not all *that* responsible, and they are definitely not bland. As I write this, the second Mississippi supreme court justice in three months faces suspension, after threatening to "whip" the chief justice. (The first one was indicted for taking bribes in exchange for favorable rulings.) And there's always Roy Moore, the chief justice of the Alabama supreme court, who was finally relieved of his duties after a decade-

long fight in which he insisted on displaying the Ten Commandments in his courtroom.

Proof of our thriving identity is everywhere. Even if you
never left the house, all you'd really have to do to find it is
read the newspaper, which is what I did before writing most of
the pieces in this book. Every year, for example, the FBI re-
leases its crime statistics, and every year they confirm that we
are the most violent people in the country. We have the most
guns, but we also own the most Bibles and have the most
churches, which we attend more than anybody else. We exercise the least, but we eat the most. (According to the Centers
for Disease Control, the obesity rate in Georgia alone in-
creased by a hefty 101.8 percent between 1991 and 1999. The
residents of New Orleans are so fat, we just got a five-year,
$13 million grant from the feds to do something about it.) I
would also venture that we are more passionate about what
we eat than people in other regions. Last year I happened to
be home in Mississippi when I saw a story in the local paper
about a man who had killed his "longtime friend and cookout
buddy" because he "would not keep his hands away from the
grill." This reminded me of a similar piece from the same
paper several years earlier, reporting on the fatal stabbing of a
husband by his wife on Thanksgiving Day. They had been
fighting over the last piece of turkey, some dark meat, and the
victim had made the mistake of taking it.

These stories are great because they don't contain—or
warrant—a bunch of explanation. They speak for themselves,
so there's no need for what Keats described as "irritable reach-

ing after fact & reason." But the temptation, apparently, is hard to resist. In 1987, when V. S. Naipaul wrote *A Turn in the South,* his drive-by assessment of the culture below the Mason-Dixon line, he had a eureka moment when he claimed to finally understand what a redneck was. Now, I am from the South, and I wouldn't begin to try to explain that, but Naipaul met a guy who did, a two-bit real estate hustler from Jackson, Mississippi, who was referred to simply as Campbell and who informed the author that a redneck "is going to wear cowboy boots; he is not necessarily going to have a cowboy hat." He also told him that "the son of a bitch loves country music," will probably live in a trailer (on which he will make late payments), and prefers hunting to having sex and river catfish to farm-raised.

Once enlightened, Naipaul professed to finding "new poetry" at the sight of a redneck with the bill of his baseball cap "turned down just so," not to mention the "bandeaux or sweat bands on the foreheads of the women drivers of redneck-style pickup trucks." Bandeaux notwithstanding, I have found plenty of poetry in my landscape and even, occasionally, in the behavior of a redneck. However, I think the latter is a whole lot more complicated and harder to define than Naipaul's guide would lead us to believe, although some of his clues are not far off the mark. I prefer to live by the rule of the late Justice Potter Stewart: I'll know one when I see one. Here again, the newspaper is instructive. In 1987, when Lemuel "Junior" Boyer, an oil refinery worker from LaPlace, Louisiana, won a $24.83 million PowerBall jackpot, the New Orleans *Times-Picayune* quoted him as saying, "I'm just taking it one day at a time." Then he added, "I'm sure I'll buy a new truck."

Rednecks, like most of us, are better off speaking for—and defining—themselves. A few years ago a friend of mine went to a wedding in Mississippi, where she introduced herself to a member of the bride's family whom she did not know. When she asked him what he did for a living, he told her he was in the "used grease" business—a succinct enough response that, like David Duke's Baby Ruth for breakfast, pretty much tells you all you need to know. Equally illuminating was a recent article in *The Times-Picayune* about a species of giant jellyfish from Australia that has somehow made its way to Louisiana, where it is wreaking havoc with the already troubled shrimping industry. Simply put, the jellyfish smother the bait fish in the shrimpers' nets but somehow avoid getting caught up in them themselves. Blackie Campo, who operates a shrimp boat with his grandson Kenny Jr., offered a theory about how "these things" elude capture: "They got some kind of sonar connected to 'em or something," he told the paper. "That's what I think anyway, and that's good enough for me."

"That's what I think anyway, and that's good enough for me." A society in which a healthy percentage of the population operates by that logic is either terrifying or vastly entertaining, depending on your point of view. Taken to extremes, it results in what my friend Jim Dees calls Peckerwood Mayhem. (In my house we explain the difference between a peckerwood and a redneck by saying that a redneck aspires—he wants a gold Rolex and a Dodge Ramcharger and a house that looks like Tara—but a peckerwood is too pitiful to aspire; he

can't even fix the car or the lawn mower or the washing machine that has been sitting in his front yard for the last five years. But we might be reaching a bit too much ourselves—I think the real reason I use the term "peckerwood" is because I love to say it.)

You could make the case that Peckerwood Mayhem is pretty much what we've had since the get-go. One serious theory holds that what has long set us apart is the predominance in our region of the Celtic population (people of Scottish, Irish, Scotch-Irish, and Welsh origins). At the beginning of the Civil War, the South's population was three-quarters Celtic, compared with the same percentage of English people in New England and the upper Midwest. Celts as a rule are said to: love the land, disdain hard work, drink recklessly, engage in outdoor recreation with gusto, and disregard the law—especially when settling matters they consider to be questions of honor or private disputes (as in who gets the last piece of dark meat). These days most people don't contemplate their roots much (unless they live in those bastions of ancestor worship, Natchez and Charleston), but it is probably no accident that the two countries in which I most immediately felt at home were Ireland and Kenya. (We also historically have the highest percentage of African Americans—in Washington County, Mississippi, where I grew up, African Americans make up 70 percent of the population.)

Another serious theory about what sets us apart has been put forth eloquently and forcefully by C. Vann Woodward, who points to what he calls "the burden of Southern history," our singularly "un-American encounter with history, with defeat, failure and poverty." In other words a war was fought on our very own soil and we lost it. This is a more intangible thing than how many firearms we own or how many pork chops we eat, but our defeat and subsequent impoverishment and occupation and general humiliation at the hands of Yankees marks us still. We have felt something, albeit filtered through generations, that no other Americans have. I once asked an intelligent friend of mine, a longtime observer of our native land, why he thought people down here drink so much, and he replied with a straight face, "Because we lost the war."

We did indeed lose the war, and people do tend to enjoy their whiskey, but, remarkably, our rate of alcoholism is well below the national average—as is our rate of mental illness and suicide. (Of course, our mental illness rate could be low because we don't necessarily define it the same way everybody else does. As many of these pieces will show, to simply lose one's mind is not considered all that much of a big deal.) Anyway, I think our general good mood comes from having long ago learned to take our humor and joy wherever we can find it (occupation and humiliation, not to mention poverty and isolation, will do that to you). We have a large capacity for entertaining ourselves—and as some folks down here would say, "It don't take much."

The title of this book is itself evidence of that ability. Every year since 1930, a turtle race known officially as the Lepanto Terrapin Derby has been run on a sixty-foot racecourse in downtown Lepanto, Arkansas, a farming town of about two thousand people forty miles northwest of Memphis, Tennessee. The derby only lasts about fifteen to twenty minutes, but the festival staged around it goes on all day and usually features a performance by an Elvis impersonator and, of course, the crowning of the Turtle Derby Queen. Arkansas is also the home of Miss Pink Tomato, who reigns over the annual festival celebrating the signature crop of Warren, Arkansas, undeterred by political correctness or feminist complaints. My friend Jenny Pugh's mother was Little Miss Pink Tomato more than fifty years ago—she rode her tricycle in the parade and still remembers it fondly. Like I said, we take our fun where we find it, and making sport of turtles or celebrating tomatoes—not to mention the beauty of our women—is usually more than enough to do the trick.

Sometimes it doesn't even take that much. When I was a child I asked my father and his friend Bill "Nick" Nicholson what they talked about on their early evening car rides around town. "Well," my father said, "mostly we talk about what dogs might be thinking." And then they both laughed, but not because he was kidding. I was reminded of that about ten years ago, when I myself was taking a ride down Greenville's main street at dusk. I was listening to *Prairie Home Companion* on the radio—which was broadcast that particular year from a theater in New York City—and Chet Atkins was the musical guest. He played an amazing version of the Beatles' "Here, There, and Everywhere" in which he somehow played the bass, rhythm, and melody all by himself on the guitar. When he got through, there was polite applause, and Chet waited, and then he said, "Damn, when I do that out there in the heartland, people throw their babies up in the air." I started laughing out loud. For all its many faults, I'm glad I came back to a place where the babies are still flying.

Queen of the Turtle Derby

and Other Southern Phenomena

Mysterious Ways

In the spring of 1997, a devastating tornado blew through Arkansas, and the governor, a Baptist minister and former president of the Arkansas Baptist State Convention named Mike Huckabee, refused to sign legislation that referred to it as an "act of God." "It seemed unreasonable," Governor Huckabee said, "that the one time government acknowledged God's existence would be in response to something that killed twenty-five people. The brokenness of the world has had cataclysmic effects, which includes the weather getting bad. But a natural disaster does not mean that God says, 'Today I think I'll kill some twins in Arkadelphia and rip their bodies apart.'"

The governor apparently has not read chapters six and seven of Genesis, in which God Himself said He was sorry He ever made any of us and announced his intention to wipe us all, man and beast, off the face of the earth, after which "the waters prevailed upon the earth a hundred and fifty days." There's some more bad weather and a whole bunch of pestilence throughout the Old Testament, but Huckabee said he knew God wouldn't do anything so "destructive."

Members of the legislature disagreed and pointed out that the term "act of God" had been around ever since there had been insurance and maybe even before, and at first refused to change the language of the bill. They also got their feelings hurt by the implication that the governor was more holy than they, or at least more vigilant on questions of theology. "I'm just as much of a Baptist as he is," declared Representative Shane Broadway, whose district had been particularly hard hit. In the end, nobody wanted to hear any more about it and "act of God" was replaced with "natural causes" so that the governor would go on and sign the bill and unleash some much-needed relief money to those people of Arkadelphia whom "the brokenness of the world" did not kill but whose homes it destroyed.

Now, I have to say that I am with the legislature on this one. Everybody knows that "natural causes" are those things that kill a person who is about ninety-eight years old in his or her sleep. "Natural causes" is not a phrase dramatic enough to describe what happens when a whole trailer park is blown across the county line. Furthermore, I think if I watched my trailer being blown across the county line, I would feel like what had happened to me was a definite, big-time act of God.

Of course, Southerners tend to think that pretty much everything is an act of God. It's easier than trying to figure out why we lost the war, why we remain generally impoverished and infested with mosquitoes and snakes and flying termites, why there is in fact "brokenness" in our world as well as plenty of tornadoes and floods and hurricanes and ice storms and hundred-percent humidity levels. Hell, it's easier than trying to figure out what made the battery go dead or who locked the keys in the car. In Mississippi alone there are more churches per capita than any other state; God looms pretty large. Also, most of us are disinclined to blame ourselves for anything.

A wise friend of mine from Louisiana once observed that Southerners can explain almost everything that is wrong with their bodies as well as their various machines and appliances with the phrases "backed up," "shorted out," or "blew out." These usually will be followed by the words "on him." As in, "You know, his engine just blew out on him."

My engine blew out on me once at the drive-through window of a Steak 'n Shake in Orlando, Florida. After I pushed the car across the street to the Texaco, the man there asked me when was the last time I had changed my oil. I told him I'd never changed my oil—I didn't know you were supposed to. After he had recovered sufficiently to speak, he looked at me and said, "Ma'am, if this car was a child, you'd be in jail." He was not trying to be funny. The look on his face made me realize that when people asked me what happened to my car, I should under no circumstances tell them that it hadn't occurred to me to change the oil in eight years. So instead I said,

"You know, that engine just blew out on me." And every single person I said that to would become immediately sympathetic, as though something exactly like that had happened to them at least once, and they'd say, "It did? It just blew out on you, huh?" And I'd say, "Yeah, it just blew out on me." Then we'd shake our heads and wonder how such a thing could possibly have happened.

Another friend of mine once called me to tell me about a mutual acquaintance of ours who had almost died because "his blood just backed up on him and he liked to choke to death." That is, sort of, what went on, but what had led up to that event was that the fellow in question drank a super-human amount of whiskey for almost thirty years until his liver simply ceased to do what my dictionary says your liver is supposed to do, which is "act in the formation of blood." However, my friend rather touchingly related the story to me—and indeed perceived it—as something that just up and happened as opposed to something that was brought on by years of living like a self-destructive maniac.

Sometimes, though, something does just up and happen that is genuinely hard to explain, like the fact that on May 11, 1894, in Bovina, Mississippi, a gopher turtle measuring six by eight inches and entirely encased in ice fell out of the sky along with the hail, an event my Mississippi almanac lists as the state's all-time "most unusual weather occurrence." Well, yeah. There is no point in trying to figure out how that could've happened. So we don't.

By necessity, I think most Southerners subscribe to Keats's

concept of negative capability. They know that "man is capable of being in uncertainties, Mysteries, doubts, without any irritable reaching after fact & reason." Yankees have a harder time with this. Ten years ago John Shelton Reed (no relation) wrote a hilarious column in which he offered "Reed's Rule for Successful Adjustment to the South," which was "Don't think that you know what's going on."

If you are not comfortable simply "being in uncertainties" or figuring that God's responsible for whatever's going on, there's always that old standby, the devil. He is most often employed immediately after you do something you know for sure you are absolutely not supposed to do. I was once at a ceremony in Washington, where, in a corny attempt to build a bit of goodwill with the powerful chairman of the Senate Foreign Relations committee, then Secretary of State Madeleine Albright gave then North Carolina senator Jesse Helms a T-shirt that said SOMEBODY IN THE STATE DEPARTMENT LOVES ME. When she presented it to him, the senator asked a flustered Albright to prove it—in front of hundreds of people—by giving him a kiss, which she did. When I saw Helms afterward, he grinned and said, "You know, the devil makes you do things."

That is undoubtedly true, though it was not the devil who made twenty people from Floydada, Texas, shuck all their worldly possessions, including their money, their clothes, and their license plates, cram themselves into a 1990 Pontiac Grand Am, and drive to Vinton, Louisiana. When they hit a tree on Vinton's main street, fifteen naked adults got out of the car and five naked children got out of the trunk. The driver, a Pentecostal preacher who was related to all the passengers, told the police chief the Lord had told them to do it. I wonder what Mike Huckabee would think about that. Me, I think it's the only explanation. I'm certainly not thinking about searching after any fact or reason.

Eat Here

The other day I saw where John Egerton had said, "The South, for better or worse, has all but lost its identity as a separate place." Well, first of all, it would certainly be for worse. But what really had me disturbed is that even though Egerton wrote *The Americanization of Dixie*, he also wrote the seminal *Southern Food* so he should know better. Our identity is safe. And anybody who has ever been to another place and tasted the food there knows it.

I was born in Greenville, Mississippi, and the first solid foods I remember putting in my mouth were a hot tamale from Doe's Eat Place, a Gulf oyster on the half shell, a barbecue sandwich with slaw from Sherman's Grocery Store, and a piece of hot-water cornbread from my grandmother's kitchen in Nashville, Tennessee. Now, if I had been born anywhere else, these are not among the first things I would have been given. (Especially not the tamale. Don't ask me why hot tamales are such a staple in the Mississippi Delta—all I know is that they took hold in the black community and, like most other things, spilled over into the white. Strangely, this is not mentioned in *The Encyclopedia of Southern Culture*, which does manage to include all our other favorite foods, from Goo Goo Clusters to grits.) Also, if the South had really become so Americanized, I would no longer be able to eat any of these things as often as I do. (Although I do eat less of Sherman's barbecue these days because Charles Sherman started serving it sliced rather than chopped, which is irritating, and Sherman's is now a restaurant instead of a grocery that dished up food in the back, which I miss. However, it does still serve some of the best fried chicken in the world. Charles himself fried me 150 pieces of it for a party one New Year's Eve.)

In the year I was born, 1960, nonfarm households in the South spent two and a half times the national average on cornmeal and twice the average on lard. I don't know what the current numbers are, but I do know that we eat more of the following than anybody else: country ham, gumbo, grits, greens, okra, sliced tomatoes, tomato aspic, pimento cheese, chess pie, Lane cake, Lord Baltimore cake, Frito chili pies from Sonic, and Robert E. Lee cake. The "Americanization" crowd will point out that these days we also eat sushi and that even Naomi Judd's short-lived restaurant in Nashville featured such Asian-fusion items as "grilled shrimp with lime ginger sauce" on its menu. And they will say that it is possible to get okra and greens and gumbo in restaurants in New York, but these are places with names like Live Bait, where the food is treated as a trendy oddity and is served along with bad mint juleps in phony Mason jars. (Another native son wrote that he didn't think Southerners drank mint juleps much anymore except at the Kentucky Derby. I have never been to the Kentucky Derby, but in my refrigerator at this very moment there is a real Mason jar full of mint-steeped sugar syrup, which I realize is not the same as muddling fresh mint and sugar in a glass, but I like to be prepared for crowds.)

The point is that while our eating habits may have become slightly more sophisticated (as have the rest of the country's), Southerners actually still eat okra and all the rest of that stuff all the time, and in huge amounts. We eat it at home or in restaurants with names like Doe's and Jim's Cafe and Mrs. Nick's (Mrs. Nick's, in Winona, Mississippi, sells the best barbecued pork chops I have ever tasted, along with phenomenally light hot cornbread and three vegetables, all for $2—or $3 for a "men's portion") or at the superlative Four Way Grill in Memphis. And to go with it, we drink a whole lot of iced tea. In high WASP strongholds like Nashville's Belle Meade, housemen in white jackets still make tea with secret combinations of pineapple juice, orange juice, and mint. But most everywhere else below the Mason-Dixon line you have only two choices: sweet or unsweet. Sweet tea was once referred to by *Hee Haw*'s Reverend Grady Nutt as "forty-weight tea," and it invariably comes in those oversize crinkly glasses, the kind that came in the Duz detergent boxes Dolly Parton used to hawk on the *Porter Wagoner Show*. Country musician Marty Stuart told me he was so worried he wouldn't be able to survive without sweet tea while on tour in Europe, he had boxes of the fixings shipped over.

Waitresses in Portland, Oregon, or Belfast, Maine, will not ask, "Sweet or unsweet?" when you order tea. You may not even get tea at all. And if you were to go over to somebody's house for a real drink in either of those places, odds are that you would not be passed a plate of cheese straws, that magical combination of Cheddar cheese, flour, butter, and cayenne pepper usually made by somebody's aunt or maid or some local little old lady who layers them in waxed paper in white cardboard boxes tied up neatly with string. Also, if you are anywhere besides the South, you will probably not have the opportunity to consume an entirely gelatin-based menu. My mother once had houseguests for a week, and by the second day she had served so many congealed items that one of the visitors complained that his blood was starting to congeal in his veins. He had already eaten tomato aspic, crabmeat mousse, cranberry salad made with lemon Jell-O, strawberry mousse, and charlotte russe. In *Gourmet of the Delta*, a cookbook put together by the Episcopal churchwomen of Leland and Hollandale, Mississippi, there are seventy-seven salad recipes and fifty-eight of them call for either Jell-O or unflavored gelatin. I didn't even count the desserts.

But it's not just the food itself that is different, it's our attitude toward it. This can best be illustrated by the names of Junior League cookbooks in the North—pompous, uptight titles like *Posh Pantry* (Kankakee, Illinois) or *Culinary Creations* (Kingston, New York)—compared with the unabashedly affectionate *Talk About Good!* (Lafayette, Louisiana) and *Come on In!* (Jackson, Mississippi). Cookbooks in the South outsell everything else but the Bible.

When Southerners are not cooking or eating, we're talking about food, arguing about it, going to get it, taking it somewhere, or inviting people over to have it. I live part of the time in New York, and in all the years I have been there, I have been wined and dined in some swell places, but I can count on one hand the number of people who have actually cooked lunch or dinner for me in their homes, and two of them don't count because they're from the South. Southerners can't stand to eat alone. If we're going to cook up a mess of greens, we want to eat them with a mess of people. We like to talk while we eat so we are forever asking people to stay for lunch, stay for supper, sit down for a piece of pie and a cup of coffee, or a drink and some sausage cheese balls.

Last week I was in New Orleans, where I also live, and I hadn't been there for an hour before my friend Peter Patout called me up and asked me to come over and eat. He had bought some shrimp by the side of the road and boiled them with corn and onions and potatoes. We covered the table with newspapers, fixed a drink, and ate. The next day he called again and asked if I wanted to eat the rest of those shrimp in some Creole sauce for lunch, and I did. While we were eating lunch, Peter's cook, Grace, was cooking chicken stew to leave for supper (it is seriously one of the best things I have ever eaten) and enjoying her own lunch of fried skins off the chicken. She gave me a bite and I remembered why I eat fried chicken. If I hadn't had to leave town, I would've gone back again for the stew.

Sometimes I wonder how people have time to do anything else. We cook for fun, we cook for love, we cook to show off, we cook when we flat just don't know what else to do. My father tells a story about a Sunday just after he and my mother had gotten married and they were driving past a new warehouse that he had built. He noticed that it was flooded, so he pulled the car over, jumped out in the rain, and yelled at my mother to go on home. My mother's own father was not given to many sudden acts and had a normal job as an insurance executive, so she got nervous, and by the time my father got home (after much sweeping of water and passing of a bottle), she had made two pies.

I called off my wedding once and a friend of my mother's, who didn't know yet whether the cancellation was good news or bad, simply brought her a hot loaf of bread. We use food to sympathize and to celebrate. We give it as presents and peace offerings. Everywhere else in America people use cash, but we use food to bribe people. I once got out of a speeding ticket in Beulah, Mississippi, by promising to bring the justice of the peace there a pecan pie from Sherman's. As every Southerner knows, a good pecan pie, especially hot with some whipped cream or ice cream melting off it, is better than money.

My mother can sound downright sexual talking about pecan pie, as most Southerners can about most food. My friend Simpson Hemphill from Carrollton, Mississippi, recently ended his description of a dessert of soda crackers and melted chocolate that his mama used to make him with the words "Oh my Lord, it would make you hurt yourself. Oh Lord, it was good." It wasn't like we were hungry. When he lapsed into the memory of "that little salt on those crackers with that chocolate candy," he had just served us a lunch of fried chicken, chicken salad, salmon salad, cucumbers and onions that had been soaking in vinegar and sugar, tomato tart, homemade bread-and-butter pickles, stuffed eggs, and Dr Pepper. But food leads to memories of more food, and if you're too full to eat anymore, you might as well keep talking about it.

The other day my mother and I were lying on the beach. Since we were both attempting to be on diets, we entertained ourselves by talking about the fried apricot pies and sliced tomato sandwiches with homemade mayonnaise on white bread cut into rounds that her childhood cook Eleanor used to make, and the shad roe on toast that her grandfather ate every Sunday it was in season. That reminded me of the creamed chicken on toast my grandmother used to make me on Sunday nights, and the coffee ice cream and homemade chocolate sauce that hardened on it for dessert, and then we just had to stop.

In *Albion's Seed*, a terrific book about the early British settlers in America, David Hackett Fischer writes that "among both high born and humble folk, eating was a more sensual experience in Virginia than in Massachusetts. There was nothing in the Chesapeake colonies to equal the relentless austerity of New England's 'canonical dish' of cold baked beans." Hell no, the Virginians were busy eating chicken fricassees made with "a pint of claret, a pint of oysters and a dozen egg yolks" instead. Fischer primarily concerns himself with the "foodways" of the eighteenth century, but a quick glance at the current Junior League cookbooks of Massachusetts and Virginia reveals the same contrast between austerity and sensuality today. In *A Taste of New England*, produced by the Junior League of Worcester, Massachusetts, the desserts include pumpkin bars and Grape-Nuts Pudding. The Richmond Junior League's *Virginia Seasons*, on the other hand, offers chocolate chess pie, brown sugar pie, Martha Washington's Great Cake (among its sixteen ingredients are a pound of butter, ten eggs, and a cup of brandy), and My Aunt Margie's Better Than Sex—layered bar cookies made from Philadelphia Cream Cheese, instant chocolate pudding, instant vanilla pudding, Hershey bars, Cool Whip, and pecans. The prepared foods in that last recipe are what Damon Lee Fowler, in his scholarly and wonderful *Classical Southern Cooking*, says has contributed to the watering down—indeed the "destruction"—of the cuisine of the Old South. However, just because it is not "classical" doesn't mean it's not Southern. Southerners do very different things with those packages and bottles than Yankees.

Take Triscuits and cream cheese. Triscuits are a Yankee invention, and the cream cheese I buy has Philadelphia in its very name, but these two items are mainstays of the Southern larder. Not long ago I was talking with my friend, the writer Henry Allen, who was born in New Jersey but is nonetheless extraordinarily brilliant on most subjects, and somehow we got on the subject of Triscuits, which he said he loved with cream cheese as much as I did.

So I asked him what he put on it. "Put on what?"

"The cream cheese, you idiot."

And there was a pause before he said, "Nothing."

I was stunned. You would never see a naked block of cream cheese in the South. It will always be coated with one of at least three delicious things: Pickapeppa Sauce, Jezebel Sauce (pineapple preserves, hot mustard, apple jelly, and horseradish), or pepper jelly. I told him this but he clearly had no idea what I was talking about, which is not surprising when you consider that he also contends that catfish and grits have no taste. I explained that when you put those two things together on your fork and all the grease and butter and salt starts to run together and the crunchy cornmeal crust of the catfish mixes with the creamy texture of the grits, there are very few things better. He said, "You mix them up?"

Certainly you mix them up, but this is another thing. Yankees like stuff (everything, not just food) discrete, clear, easily identifiable—black and white, not gray. Southerners are more comfortable with mystery and mingling (except historically, of course, in matters of race). Witness Huck Finn's dissatisfaction with the Widow Douglas's proper supper: "Everything was cooked by itself." He preferred it, he said, when "things got mixed up and the juice kind of swaps around, and the things go better."

It is fear of things like unadorned cream cheese (or, indeed, lack of sweet tea) that motivates Southerners to take their food with them wherever they go—or at least to try and replicate it. Displaced Southern people are always getting together to eat black-eyed peas on New Year's Day, and turkey with cornbread dressing on Thanksgiving in countries where no one's ever even heard of Thanksgiving. On the other hand, I once brought a whole black truffle from Manhattan's Dean & DeLuca home to Mississippi, and shaved it into some mashed potatoes. Nobody even noticed, and I realized the futility of trying to outdo what was already perfect. So these days I only tote things out: Doe's tamales tied in bundles and stored upright in their "juice" in old coffee cans, frozen one-pound packages of crawfish tails packed in dry ice, real cornmeal and not that nasty mix. A few summers ago a friend and I had a party in the English countryside at which we served daube glacé with homemade mayonnaise, shrimp étouffée, crawfish rémoulade, and Paul Prudhomme's three-layer mocha chocolate cake with sugar and Karo syrup. It wasn't easy but we did it. My cohostess, from Atlanta, has been known to travel around with dried red beans and grits and Zatarain's filé in her suitcase, and I don't blame her. The last time I had a dinner party in New York I had to go to seven grocery stores before I found some black-eyed peas, and I never did find any ladyfingers. The dinner was in honor of my friend André Leon Talley, who is originally from North Carolina. André lived for a time in Paris, at the Ritz Hotel, and he still regularly lunches with various Rothschilds, who, I imagine, must have some pretty good chefs, but all André ever wants me to make him is fried chicken and squash casserole and black-eyed peas with rice.

The night before it closed for good, a friend of mine from the Delta had dinner at Joel Robuchon's restaurant in Paris. It was considered one of the best restaurants in the world, so I asked her if her meal there was the best one she ever ate. "Nope," she said. So I asked her what *was* the best meal she ever ate, and she said it was years ago at her grandmother's house: sliced homegrown tomatoes and hot cornbread with the mustard-and-Jerusalem-artichoke pickle relish that her grandmother and her aunts put up every year. There is a famous story about William Faulkner and Katherine Anne Porter dining at a swanky restaurant in Paris. After draining the burgundy and the port, Faulkner fiddled with his glass and said, "Back home the butter beans are in, the speckled ones." Katherine Anne Porter stared off into the middle distance and said, simply, "Blackberries."

This is a foolproof exercise. If you ask any Southerner to name the best meal he ever ate, he will invariably recall something that his mama or grandmama or his mama's or grandmama's cook fixed at home. If you ask a Yankee about the best meal he ever ate, he will invariably name a four-star, impossible-to-get-into restaurant and usually not even mention the actual food. I put the question to a famous Yankee novelist and he said he couldn't decide between Daniel in Manhattan and a restaurant neither of us could remember how to pronounce in Florence. Now Daniel is unquestionably a remarkable restaurant, and I absolutely love to be taken there. But I'm on the side of the novelist's ex-wife, who is from Nashville. When I asked her the same question, she said, "Smothered chicken, hot-water cornbread, and fried corn." Hot-water cornbread is cornmeal mixed with hot water and shaped into patties and fried in lard, and fried corn is not actually fried at all but scraped off the cob straight into an iron skillet and boiled (this is the archaic use of the word "fried") in grease and its own milk. Some cooks let a crust form on the bottom and then stir the crusty bits into the corn. Either way it is delicious, and I interrupted my friend to comment appreciatively on that fact but she stopped me.

"I'm not finished. For dessert there was caramel cake and custard pie."

I called my editor in New York and asked, "What's the best meal you ever ate?"

"Daniel, on my birthday."

"Yeah, but what did you eat?"

"Um, lamb shanks, I think."

So I called my best friend Jessica in Greenville, and she remembered exactly what her favorite meal was because it was the one she had just finished eating: "Fried catfish, okra and tomatoes, corn on the cob, turnip greens, lima beans, mashed potatoes, cornbread, sliced tomatoes, green onions, and tea."

"Jesus. Who made it?"

"Mama, Granny, and Malvina." Her mother, her grandmother, and the cook.

Then her daddy got on the phone. "Baby, you gotta come down here and taste my beer chicken." Stupidly, I asked him how he made it. "You just gotta come down here and see."

So I called Jessica back later and asked her about the chicken, which I figured must be marinated in beer. Nope. Beer chicken is a whole chicken rubbed with Cajun spices and "stuffed" with a full, open beer can. The beer can, with a sip or two drunk from it so it won't spill over, is inserted upright into the chicken's cavity, at which point the chicken looks like a fat old man sitting on a stump. Then the whole thing is placed on a grill with the hood closed until the chicken is done. "It's really good," Jessica said with complete seriousness, explaining that the beer steams the chicken from the inside. "It makes the chicken really tender." It is so good, in fact, that her daddy, the inimitable Howard Brent, got a guy to make a contraption that will hold six beer cans in a circle to fit on the grill. Now Howard grills half a dozen chickens at a time. I can hardly wait. "Only a man could've invented that," said Jessica.

I corrected her: "Only a Southern man."

Trigger Happiness

When the FBI released its preliminary crime statistics for 1996, "serious crime"—which includes stuff like murder, rape, assault, and car theft—had dropped by as much as 8 percent in every region of the country. Except in the South, where "serious crime" was up by 2 percent. It was also noted that although only a third of the nation's population lives in the South, 42 percent of all homicides happen here. Our reputation for violence and criminal disorder remains firmly rooted in fact. Or as my friend Simpson Hemphill is always telling me, "There is nothing new in this world."

That is certainly true of this particular subject. During the Revolutionary War, soldiers from Connecticut threatened to leave the front if they had to serve alongside the soldiers from Virginia because the brawls the Southern boys waged among themselves were far too frequent and brutal. In the 1870s, when a man named H. V. Redfield conducted the first study of comparative homicide rates, he found that the homicide rate of South Carolina was ten times that of Massachusetts. H. C. Brearley made another study in the 1920s and found that the seven states with the highest per capita homicide rates were Southern.

I don't think they had sociologists in the 1870s or even in the 1920s, but we damn sure have them now, and they have the usual stuff to say about the latest round of numbers. Southerners are violent because we are: poor, racist, under-educated, alienated, oppressed. Historians point to our fron-tier mentality and the legacy of the dueling code. Or they say we're taking our passionate belief in states' rights to an irra-tional extreme. In other words, we think it's not just our right but our duty to settle conflicts personally, and without a lot of persnickety input from law enforcement authorities. *USA Today* went so far as to cite the heat as a possible factor. But our tendency toward violence doesn't really warrant a whole lot of heavy analysis. We shoot more people because we have the most guns.

Mr. Redfield reached this conclusion when he was run-ning around South Carolina. He reported that "assaults on honor and political arguments" frequently resulted in murder because everybody carried a weapon. This is still true. I don't think I know anybody in the South who doesn't carry, or at least own, a gun. In Mississippi, for example, under the "gun-slinger law," everybody except convicted felons can pay for the privilege of carrying their guns wherever they like, as long as it's not a church or a courtroom. This means that quite a lot of people have guns ready and available at all times. Articles in the newspapers almost invariably end descriptions of shootings with sentences like this: "Then he picked up a gun and shot him." I mean, these articles never say, "Then he walked to the cedar chest"—or to the dresser, or to the locked closet—"where he got his gun." Instead an article might recount a murder at the breakfast table, which means, apparently, that the average Southerner sets his table with a fork, a knife, and a gun. Also, I don't think the guy who shoots his girlfriend over a bowl of Cheerios is thinking: "I'm shaped by the frontier. I've got these impulses racing through me. I might have to blow her head off." He's thinking: "I am so damned tired of listening to this woman bitch at me." (This is what qualifies these days as an "assault on honor.") If he happens to have a gun on hand, he doesn't have to listen to anybody.

Jerry Lee Lewis shot his drummer once, but he didn't mean to. He meant to shoot the lamp. Country singer Trace Adkins's wife shot him during a fight over his broken promise to quit drinking beer. Mrs. Adkins, according to *People* magazine, "grabbed the family .38 from the top of the fridge" and shot her husband through both lungs and both ventricles of his heart. (He lived.)

Elvis had several guns on him when he visited the White House. I'm sure he didn't even think about it. He's going out, he's got his guns. I never saw Coatee Jones, the woman who raised me, when she didn't have a .22 in her purse, and I saw her every day for sixteen years. Women tend to carry their guns in their purses. Men tend to keep them in the glove compartment or their boots. Both sexes carry a gun because they believe that during the course of any given day they might have to use it, and that if they do use it they won't have a choice. As in: "You know, I had to shoot that guy." Murder, then, becomes something "tragic" rather than something very, very bad that you are not, under any circumstances, supposed to commit.

It was, for example, a tragedy last year when a resident of New Orleans shot and killed a man he thought was trying to steal his truck, which was parked down the street from his house. The truck owner happened to be looking out his kitchen window at the time, and since he had his gun nearby, he fired it. It was also a tragedy a few Halloweens ago when a guy in Baton Rouge shot and killed a Japanese exchange student who was trick-or-treating, and therefore, approaching his front door. The homeowner explained that he had to shoot the kid because he was "moving kinetically."

Protecting your property is very big in the South. There would still be a gun in the house I grew up in except that one night after my mother and I watched a movie about a traveling executioner, she couldn't sleep and thought she heard somebody outside. My father had given her a .44 Magnum to keep in her bedside table drawer when he was out of town. So she picked it up and accidentally blew a hole in the bedroom wall the size of a garbage can lid. The bullet kept going, through the bathroom door and through the door to the linen closet, where it was finally waylaid by a stack of monogrammed towels. After that she made my father take all the guns out of the house, but I know he still thinks they are useful. When he visited me at an apartment I had awhile back in New Orleans—not the most secure of places—he didn't remark on its amazingly high ceilings or the marble mantelpieces or the exquisite plaster molding. His sole comment before he walked out was: "You need to get a gun."

Though random murders and street crime are on the rise in the South, Southerners still tend to kill people they know. The South leads the nation in murders of lovers, spouses, and other relatives (though we don't kill our children any more than most people do). But really, we'll shoot just about anything. There is a country song called "Bubba Shot the Jukebox Last Night," and everybody knows Elvis shot his TV. My best friend once had a date with a guy named Lee, and they were driving around in a cotton field drinking beer and getting stoned (which is what you did on dates). After a while the car broke down so Lee just jumped out and shot it three times. If I owned a gun I know I would've shot my computer at least a hundred times by now, and I definitely would've blown a hole in my stereo after it ate its twenty-ninth cassette last week. Let's face it, the one thing the historians get right is that we've been messed with so much for so long now that we take everything personally. If everybody else is out to get us, why not our appliances?

To Live and Die in Dixie

My favorite American newspaper page is the daily wire-service roundup in *USA Today* called "Across the USA: News from Every State." It provides a steady stream of evidence that there is still a South, despite the tedious efforts of underemployed, mostly Southern academics who churn out endless studies telling us that the South is over as a separate place. (Northerners rarely make these pronouncements because they know we're not like them.) The theory is that strip malls, fast food, suburbs, cable TV—not to mention the end of the South's political isolation more than thirty years ago—have made us all but indistinguishable from the rest of America. Or that since most of our national leaders now come from the South—as do two of the things most often cited as causes of the country's increasing homogenization,

CNN and Wal-Mart—the rest of America is becoming more like us.

I have kept a file of the *USA Today* page for years, so that I will always have on hand brief but forceful proof that neither assertion is true. For example, on the same day in 1994 that the Tennessee state senate in Nashville okayed a bill that would allow handguns to be used in self-defense—even by convicted felons—a citizens group in Seattle, Washington, put forth an initiative that would increase the prison term of anyone using a gun to commit a crime. On August 14, 1995, the big news in Colorado was that the citizens were upset about the noise coming from the Denver International Airport, while in Arkansas, a six-year-old girl shot herself in the chest with a gun she found under her mother's pillow, and in Middlesboro, Kentucky, police were probing the death of a woman who died of a snakebite inflicted during Sunday services at the Full Gospel Tabernacle Church. It was, the paper reported, "the second church-related snake-bite death this year."

On August 4, 2000, a judge in Kansas was reprimanded for allowing his secretary to hold a second job. That same day, a judge in Arkansas was busy upholding the conviction of a preacher who had burned down his own church in hopes that it would unite his flock. And finally, on August 28, the news from Tennessee concerned Knoxville used-car dealer Lumpy Lambert's "Second Amendment Saturday." Shoppers who bought a car also got a voucher for a bolt-action, eight-millimeter deer rifle valued at $100.

If there is a theme here, it is that Southerners are still the most violent people in America, but we are also the most religious.* (The stats bear this out: In 1999, violent crime was way down in every region of the country but the South. Southerners own more guns per capita, but we also have the most churches, and the most churchgoers—Southerners attending church once a week outnumber Northerners almost two to one.) This has been true for some time. Confederate general Stonewall Jackson was such a devout observer of the Sabbath he wouldn't dare mail a letter if he thought it might be in transit on Sunday, but he didn't much care what day it was when he fought. One of his men wrote that Jackson "would shoot a man at the drop of a hat, and he'd throw the hat down."

A long-standing Southern tradition encompassing religion and violence was outlawed by the Supreme Court last summer when the justices ruled that schools were no longer allowed to broadcast the Lord's Prayer before Friday-night high school football games. The ruling prompted the immediate formation of such organizations as We Still Pray, which encourage student bodies across the region to engage in a pre-kickoff "organized spontaneous outbreak of prayer" in the bleachers. To the distress of civil liberties groups, the movement has been enormously successful, which brings up another characteristic of the Southerner: We do not like to be told what to do, especially not by the federal government.

When the Supreme Court ruled twenty-three years ago that capital punishment was once again permissible, Southern states, still irritated that the court had taken the right away from them, were the first to pass laws reinstating the death penalty. Since then they have executed more people than all the other states combined. In Alabama, the electric chair is looked upon with such fondness that it has a name, "Yellow Mama."

Alabama, like its neighbors, apparently does not think "Thou shalt not kill" applies to the state. In general, however, the Ten Commandments are very popular. When a high court found that Alabama circuit judge Roy Moore's display of Moses' commandments on his courtroom wall—on plaques the judge had carved himself out of pine—violated the Constitution by promoting religion in a government setting, the governor himself rushed to the judge's defense. He said he would call out the National Guard if anyone tried to remove the plaques from the wall. Like the late Mississippi writer Willie Morris said, it's the juxtapositions that drive you crazy.

Instead of removing his plaque, he replaced it. After he was elected chief justice of the Alabama supreme court in 2000—largely because of his stand on the Commandments issue—he installed in the rotunda of the state court building a two-and-a-half-ton granite Ten Commandments monument, which became known as Roy's Rock. When, in 2003, a federal judge ordered it removed, Moore refused, and his supporters, many of whom wore T-shirts reading PROPERTY OF JESUS and SATAN IS A NERD, staged emotional rallies on the courthouse steps. "If I have to give my life for [the monument], it will never come out," declared the Reverend Harry Bunn. "I'll wrap my legs around the forklift and break my legs if necessary." Brenda Hyche, who had driven over to Montgomery from Jasper, Alabama, told *The New York Times*, "Taking it away is wrong, and this is an opportunity for God to flex his muscle." In the end the only muscles flexed were those of the five workmen who finally removed the thing and of Moore's colleagues on the bench who finally removed him.

We may not like what the feds have to say, a lot, but we do listen to God and He seems to be everywhere. A man in Lucy, Louisiana, found a cross-shaped sweet potato in his vegetable garden fifteen years ago, and in a news article celebrating the fifteenth anniversary of the find, he said that the now-shriveled potato had brought him "closer to God. You change. It's all for the better."

A few years ago in Atlanta, when a forty-one-year-old bodybuilder and mother of two was trying to decide whether to remain in her church choir or do some secular singing, she asked God for a sign. He told her to look up from the wheel of the car she was driving down Memorial Drive at a billboard for Pizza Hut. There, in a giant photograph of a forkful of spaghetti advertising the new lunch special, she saw "the Michelangelo version of Christ," whereupon, she said, "I lost my breath." Not only did she decide to stay in the church choir, she called *The Atlanta Journal-Constitution* to report what she saw. It turned out that dozens of motorists had already called, and before long, hundreds of believers clogged the road to check it out for themselves.

I plan on submitting this last news clip at the next "Is there still a South?" seminar I am forced to attend. Because I don't think the Lord is telling people from anywhere else to look for signs in Pizza Hut billboards. Or if He is, it hasn't made the papers.

Lady Killers

I grew up listening to the story of Howard Dyer's Abraham Lincoln. Dyer, the flamboyant, one-armed lawyer from my hometown of Greenville, was one of Mississippi's most famous defense attorneys. The Lincoln was the black Continental he bought with his fee for keeping Erma Abraham out of jail after she blew a hole in the top of her husband's head with a .38. The car was also a symbol of a simple truth: A woman—a white, well-dressed, churchgoing woman—in the Deep South could, generally, kill her husband and walk away.

"I don't know why people say we're chauvinists down here," my father has said more than once. "Look how nice we are to women. A woman can flat kill her husband in the state of Mississippi and get away with it."

Mrs. Abraham killed her husband in 1966 in Leland, Mississippi, a town of about five thousand people ten miles west of Greenville, and the same place where Ruth Dickins had hacked up her mama with some hedge clippers eighteen years earlier. Mrs. Dickins, who told the sheriff "a Negro" did it, actually served time—matricide is a little touchier than husband killing—but the governor commuted her life sentence after a little more than six years, and she came back to take her place in the First Baptist Church, running the nursery and teaching Sunday school. Mrs. Dickins was from a fine old Delta family, had plenty of money, was married to a well-thought-of cotton broker and planter, and lived in a big white house on the banks of Deer Creek, where the rest of the Leland gentry (including her mother) chose to reside.

In 1949, a year after her conviction, a writer from New York came down and wrote a long piece in which he made the case that the fact that such a woman had been found guilty and sent to the penitentiary was proof that the "traditions and wealth and chivalry of the Old South . . . the most potent forces in the Delta" had lost their punch. "This family . . . has tumbled from its lofty position," he wrote. "The Old South is dead now, unquestionably."

Well, not exactly. Had he stuck around, he would've seen the following evidence to the contrary.

When both of Ruth Dickins's daughters were presented to society at the Delta Debutante Ball in Greenville, Mrs. Dickins was out of jail for both occasions, thanks to two ten-day "holiday suspensions" granted her by the governor before he suspended her sentence altogether.

Erma Abraham was found not guilty based on the defense that she was the victim of her husband's "unnormal" sex acts, which made her so crazy that she didn't even remember shooting him, much less wrapping the gun up in aluminum foil and hiding it in the deep freeze. She spent sixty days in the state mental hospital at Whitfield before being released and moving to Memphis.

Two years later, in 1968, Peggy Bush told a jury in Jackson, Mississippi, that she thought she was shooting her prominent-lawyer husband with a "pop gun" (it was actually a .22). She was found not guilty after the jury deliberated for three minutes, still a record in the state.

Twenty years after that, in 1988, a Greenville pathologist, Dr. Benella Oltremari, pumped the contents of two guns into her husband's chest and was immediately slapped into a hospital room where she was protected by armed guards. She wasn't questioned about the "tragic accident" until ten days later, when the police chief finally obtained a court order to do so.

Now, I know about these women because they happened to live within a ten-mile radius of me and one another (with the exception of Peggy Bush, who lived 120 miles away in Jackson, though her sister lived in Greenville). But the examples of the South's indulgence toward the female criminal element are legion. Take the case of Susan Smith, who in 1995 drowned her children in a lake outside Union, South Carolina, and, like Ruth Dickins before her, blamed her crime on a black man. Also like Mrs. Dickins, Smith did not kill her husband, making her case a bit more problematic. The almost invariable unspoken defense of ladies who kill their husbands is that "the SOB deserved it."

"The problem," says Robert Gordon, an expert on jury selection from Dallas who helped the prosecution pick the jury for the Smith trial, "is nobody thinks those children deserved killing." Also, the town itself felt victimized and betrayed by Smith's original tale of a carjacking and kidnapping by a "black man with a gun." Still, in the end, the jury took just two and a half hours to decide not to give Smith the death penalty (even though Southerners are supposed to be more rabidly in favor of the death penalty than any people on the planet, and a *Newsweek*/CNN poll taken at the time showed that 63 percent of the people nationwide are pro–capital punishment). Smith received life instead, making her eligible for parole when she is fifty-eight. Suppose, asked Tommy Pope, the prosecutor who caught a lot of local flack for going after the death penalty in the first place, "it had been the black guy with the gun? They would've raised hell if I hadn't gone for the death penalty." Or suppose it had been her husband? "If it had been her husband," says Union radio personality Carlisle Henderson, host of *The Coffee Sippers' Gospel Hour*, "I'm afraid of what would have happened to him."

There has always been a double standard in capital cases, and not just in the South. Of the twenty thousand people lawfully executed in this country since Colonial times, fewer than four hundred of them have been women. A few months after Smith was spared the death penalty, then governor of Illinois George Ryan commuted Guin Garcia's death sentence. These days Ryan is best known for commuting the death sentences of everybody on death row on the day before he left office in 2003, but he commuted Garcia's long before he made a habit of the practice. He went out of his way to say it wasn't because she was a woman, but of course it was. Garcia's problem up until that fortunate point was that she was a poor woman of Hispanic descent in a Midwestern state or she wouldn't have been on death row in the first place. She smothered her child (who was about to be remanded to the man who had molested Garcia herself from the time she was six) and killed her husband (who was also her pimp) in a botched robbery. Her upbringing was arguably more tragic than that of Susan Smith (whose father killed himself and whose stepfather, with whom she subsequently had an affair, began fondling her when she was sixteen), but unlike Smith, Garcia was not lucky enough to be in a place where the entire town bent over backward to give her the benefit of the doubt. Smith's lawyer based her defense on her tendencies toward suicide and it worked. "I'm still convinced that she had planned to get in the car and die with those kids," Carlisle Henderson told me. "There were rumors that her husband was going to get those kids and she didn't want nobody else to have them." Pause. "I don't know if I'm forcing myself to feel that way or not."

The fact is that we will force ourselves to feel almost anything to keep the romanticized ideal of pristine Southern womanhood intact. The desire to hold on to that myth is much stronger than a desire for truth or justice—ideals never held in much esteem down here in the first place. And to let go of it would be to admit that we lost the war, that things are different now, which nobody really wants to do. We are in denial about most things, but we are also used to living with contradictions, chief among them the mixture of politeness and violence, of extreme piety and the desire to do whatever the hell we want whenever the hell we want to do it. It is entirely possible that a woman could come home from church, put on a housecoat, and then blow her husband's brains out while he slept; there just has to be a reason.

Howard Dyer came up with a whole set of reasons why Erma Abraham did exactly that, thereby earning his fee of $10,000 in cash. (He used to say that people could be sure of two things when he walked into a courtroom: that he had been paid and that the money was already spent.) The first thing he did was put a gold crucifix around Erma Abraham's neck and get what seemed like everybody in town, including her employers at the cotton brokerage where she had been a longtime secretary, to come in and testify as to her devout Episcopalian ways and her reputation for "truth and veracity."

"She wore matching designer suits and shoes," John Webb, the county attorney who prosecuted the case, told me. "She was a tea-sipping, well-dressed lady . . . very much the outward lady, and nobody could believe she had done it."

The second thing Howard Dyer did was turn Will Abraham into a monster. Mr. Abraham was a well-liked retired mail carrier, the founding coach of the successful Leland High football team, who, according to the Greenville paper, the *Delta Democrat Times*, was "an ardent fisherman and fond of growing flowers." The only time I ever saw him was in a picture taken after he was dead, shown to me by Howard Dyer III, who had assisted his father in the case. Abraham was lying on the couch in his den in front of the television, his pipe and tobacco pouch on the table next to him. One eye behind his metal-frame glasses was open and one was closed, there was a hole at the top of his forehead, and two rivers of coagulated blood flowed from his nose. "Look what else," Howard III told me, directing my attention to the top button of his trousers, unfastened at the waist, just as his daddy had directed the jury thirty years before.

"That suggestion was made to Howard by a former deputy sheriff," said John Webb. "He told him, 'If you can get about three or four rednecks on that jury, that [undone button] will work to your advantage.' There's some vulgarity attached to that and it could offend some people. Every little nuance can be a nudge to a jury."

Actually, Howard Dyer was not very big on nuances. Mrs. Abraham told a packed—and completely stunned courtroom—that her husband had become impotent, and, afraid that he would lose her if he could not satisfy her in some other way, he began forcing her into "unnormal" sex acts, specifically cunnilingus. When that last word was printed in the paper, it was, according to then editor Hodding Carter III, for the first time. It was also almost certainly the first time most of the men on that jury had heard it said aloud. (Their eyes, according to the paper, "were fixed on the floor.")

Although in 1966 Mississippi still had a state law barring women from being seated on juries, a federal court had just thrown out a verdict in Alabama because of a similar law there. Dyer had, not surprisingly, motioned for there to be no women at all, but to be safe, the judge included a handful of women—as well as some black men—in the larger jury pool. However, the twelve male jurors ultimately seated were all white male Protestants, four of whom worked for utility companies and two of whom were well-to-do planters. After Mrs. Abraham's testimony, Philip Mansour, an attorney assisting the prosecution on behalf of the three remaining Abraham brothers, questioned how a "sixty-two-year-old man who was half-dead, half-blind, and lame . . . became a raving sex maniac," but the damage had been done. A lawyer who was in the courtroom swears to me he overheard a spectator say, "This never would have happened if she had married a white man." (Mr. Abraham was of Lebanese descent.) But mostly the jury would have been so embarrassed by it all they would have found her not guilty on the spot just to get the hell out of there.

But there was more. MRS. ABRAHAM IS VICTIM OF BRAIN IN-JURY, AMNESIA PSYCHIATRIST TELLS COURT was the headline. Just in case anybody wanted to make an issue of the fact that Mrs. Abraham had originally claimed that an intruder had shot her husband or that she had wrapped the gun in foil and hidden it in the deep freeze, a Jackson psychiatrist named Willard Waldron arrived at the Washington County courthouse in a Rolls-Royce to say that the defendant suffered from "acute brain syndrome," rendering her unable to remember certain events such as the murder. He had been paid $500 by the defense and he based his diagnosis solely on what Mrs.

Abraham had told him during the few hours that they had met, but he testified that her brain had been "jostled" during "repeated violent shaking" by her husband.

"The spectacle [Dr. Waldron] made of himself in this courtroom," Philip Mansour said in his closing arguments, "was a disgrace to the people of Mississippi, to the institutions that educated him, and to himself."

Except that it worked. "Will is destroyed in body but Erma is destroyed in mind," Dyer told the court in his own twenty-seven-minute summation. "Look at her face," he shouted before the jury box, taking his jacket off and waving his lone arm wildly toward Mrs. Abraham. "See the tragedy and pathos that's in that face. Erma Abraham is not ready to be returned to society." On June 29, 1966, one day after closing arguments were completed, and the day before fifty-eight years of widely ignored Prohibition came to an end in the state of Mississippi, the jury found Mrs. Abraham not guilty by reason of insanity. The judge explained to Mrs. Abraham that she would be held at Whitfield, the state mental hospital outside Jackson, "until your condition is improved so that you can resume your place in society."

She resumed that place just sixty days later, and in her absence it was discovered that the "rigid moral and spiritual beliefs" ascribed to her by the good Dr. Waldron did not include an aversion to stealing. Her former employers, who had paid for her bail and her defense, which included Waldron's fee, discovered that Mrs. Abraham had been embezzling tens of thousands of dollars from them for years. But when they asked

Mr. Webb, the county attorney, to take action, he reminded them that "if she was crazy when she killed her husband, she must have been crazy when she took the money."

It was hardly a surprise that a jury accepted the fact that a woman could go crazy in the face of "unnormal" sex acts, since we tend to accept that people can just go crazy without much prompting at all. When my father asked the late Mississippi senator James Eastland what had happened to a certain member of his staff, he responded, without taking his ever-present cigar out of his mouth or even changing expression, that the man in question had "lost his mind." "Oh, Senator, no," said my father, trying to summon up a suitably horrified response. "He lost his mind?" "Yes," said Eastland, and the conversation was over.

Eastland's colleague, Strom Thurmond, the late senator from South Carolina who remained in his seat until just after his one hundredth birthday, used to give a speech in which he said that if he were ever "struck insane" he hoped it would be in Washington, where no one would know the difference. He was poking fun at his age and his colleagues, of course, but the most telling thing about the remark is the phrase "struck insane." People don't just get old or grow feebleminded in his world—it is entirely possible to be a healthy, powerful senator one day and to be a lunatic the next.

Southerners do not question unexplained phenomena or the mysteries of nature, human or otherwise. This is a place, after all, where a great many livelihoods are literally at the mercy of the weather, where thousands of people still speak in tongues every Sunday. Stuff happens. So if somebody simply loses it one day and is back to normal the next, or indeed, in sixty days, we take it at face value. "She must have just snapped," said a friend and former high school classmate of Susan Smith's, as if that was explanation enough for strapping a three-year-old and a fourteen-month-old into a Mazda sedan and rolling them into a lake. "There is, in my opinion, a breaking point for everyone," explained the pastor of the St. Paul Baptist Church in Smith's hometown.

Women are deemed especially susceptible, especially for legal purposes. Dr. Benella Oltremari, the pathologist from Greenville, found out her husband, Marty Albinder, was cheating on her with his secretary and shot him five times in the chest and stomach with both a .38 and a .44 Magnum. He was taken to the Delta Medical Center but so was she. "I viewed her as seriously upset and in need of medical attention immediately after the accident," said Oltremari's lawyer, the former state legislator H. L. "Sonny" Meridith. "She wasn't in any condition to talk to the police." The hospital where she practiced said she was "in shock" and kept her in a private room with guards at the door. "We feel she could at least be arrested and processed," the police captain in charge told the newspaper, but by the time he was allowed to question her, Albinder, who now refers to himself as "Bullets," had miraculously pulled through and pronounced the whole thing a "tragic accident."

Men have been known to snap as well, most often just before women snap and kill them. Mrs. Abraham testified that on the night she shot her husband, he had appeared at the kitchen door with a terrible look on his face. "I've never seen such a look," she said. "He looked like he was crazy."

Two years later, when Peggy Bush shot her husband at their Jackson home, it was after a dinner party, and during, the newspaper made a point of noting, the telecast of the Miss America pageant. Millard Bush went to the bedroom of the couple's fourteen-year-old daughter, Pamela, yelled at her about the size of her bills at the country club, told her he didn't like the way she looked or what she wore, and said that he was going to kill her. "I don't know what made him completely snap, which is what he did, completely snap," Peggy Bush told the jury, the first in the state to finally include a woman. "His teeth were all together and his eyes were closed," she said, adding that he cursed her using words that she could bring herself to repeat only by using the initials "g.d., s.o.b., and worse." He had, she said, snapped only once before, three years earlier, after he had fallen and sustained—naturally—"a brain injury."

Ruth Dickins seems to have snapped big-time the afternoon she took the shears to her mother. Court papers show that the left side of the victim's head "was chopped all to pieces" and that the "right side was practically mutilated," two of her fingers had been severed, her skull and her elbow were fractured, and she was "hit around the head 155 to 200 times." Sixty percent of the damage had been done to the victim—who was seventy years old, weighed ninety pounds, and had been brought home from the hospital the very morning of the day she was killed—after she was already dead. Mrs.

Dickins maintained until the day she died that "a Negro" had done it—most likely, she told the sheriff, one who was angry that her mother had not let him pick the pecans off her trees—although, according to court papers, "there were no bloody tracks or other indications of the flight of any Negro from the scene of the crime." It was also noted that Mrs. Dickins seemed unusually calm in the immediate aftermath of the tragedy, that she seemed more concerned with the welfare of the kittens in her mother's garage, and, most important, that the shears had been wiped clean. It would have been unlikely, found the court, "that a Negro would have stopped to wash the shears to remove evidence of the crime."

Nonetheless, roadblocks were maintained for a week, and almost every black man in the Mississippi Delta with so much as a scratch on his hand was stopped and questioned. Finally, after two months, Mrs. Dickins was indicted, although most of the evidence had been destroyed within hours of the murder. The sheriff had allowed the bathroom to be cleaned at Mrs. Dickins's request; she had directed her maid to soak her own clothes in a washtub, and the funeral home had burned those of her mother when nobody came to get them because they smelled bad. There had been a brief flurry about the possibility of a black man on the jury—the Supreme Court had ruled that blacks had to be considered—but the lone black man tentatively accepted for service was excused after he said he wouldn't vote for the execution of a white woman even if the evidence justified it. In the end, on June 30, 1949, twelve white men found her guilty but couldn't agree on punishment, so the judge sentenced her to life in prison and she was sent to the state penitentiary at Parchman.

In her six and a half years at Parchman, she was granted the two ten-day holiday leaves as well as a three-month medical leave, arranged by her doctor, the highly respected Paul Gamble, who had written the governor saying that Mrs. Dickins had a "uterine disturbance" that caused a "swimming of the head," was under a "nervous strain," and that she was "very allergic" to the prison diet. Beginning in 1953, three petitions containing a total of 908 signatures were also sent to the governor, along with letters from three jurors who said "there was now considerable doubt in their minds concerning the crime," and one from Tony Gardenia, owner of Vince's Cafe, who wrote on stationery bearing the logo "Miller High Life, the Champagne of Beers." Finally, the governor himself came to town and held a public hearing in the Bank of Leland, at which seventy people spoke on Mrs. Dickins's behalf. The planter Charles Dean voiced the opinion that it probably would have been more suitable to have sent Mrs. Dickins to Whitfield (this lesson served Mrs. Abraham well eighteen years after Ruth Dickins killed her mother), and that there was no question in his mind that it was time for her to come home and be with her family. The governor, Hugh L. White, agreed and, citing her "great loss of weight" and her status as a model prisoner (she had taught Sunday school to her fellow inmates), granted her an "indefinite suspension" on December 9, 1955. The family took out an ad in the *Leland Progress* announcing her impending return, and she moved back to Leland and her house on Deer Creek with her husband, who had visited her every Sunday and who maintained her innocence until the day he died in 1977.

Mrs. Dickins herself died on January 22, 1996, at the age of eighty-nine from heart failure, more than forty years after her release. She had remained extremely active in church affairs, served on the board of trustees of the Hawaii Baptist Academy in Honolulu, and ran the nursery at the First Baptist Church in Leland ("the finest children's nursery of any church I've seen," said county attorney John Webb.) Her obituary in the *Delta Democrat-Times* mentioned her "pioneer Delta heritage," her graduation from Hollins College in Roanoke, Virginia, her marriage, her extensive church involvement, and her membership in the Leland Garden Club. Mourners were instructed to make memorials to the Hawaii Baptist Academy, Hollins, or the Mississippi Animal Rescue League. It did not mention her mother's murder or her time in the penitentiary, although at her funeral the preacher, the Reverend John Doler, did read the One Hundred and Third Psalm, the central point of which, he said, is that the Lord pardons our iniquities. "I never made reference to what had occurred, but the people who knew, knew where I was coming from."

After the funeral, one of her relatives told me that "Ruth was a remarkable woman if you met her halfway," and that although "circumstances happen . . . let's just remember that life is composed of chapters." Another reminded me that "there has always been some question about whether or not Ruth actually did this," and that "if she did not do it and she is protecting someone else, it ought to end. It ought to end."

A woman, in all her selfless, maternal benevolence, taking the fall for someone close to her, is a familiar theme in these cases. A famous murder in Nashville, Tennessee, involved my aunt Jane's best friend, Jean Wilson, who ran her husband, John, through with a samurai sword. Although she was charged with the crime (and, of course, acquitted), the rumor to this day in the salons of Belle Meade, the wealthy Nashville enclave where the Wilsons lived, is that she was covering up for her son. But, as in the Dickins case, there was no way to tell because most of the evidence was destroyed. Before Jean Wilson called the police, she called my aunt Jane, who came over and cleaned up and put the blood-soaked curtains in the trunk of her car. They had not, they explained, wanted the place to look such a mess if so many people were going to be trooping in and out. When the police did get there, Jean Wilson told them that she and her husband had just been horsing around on the bed with the sword, which had been hanging on the wall.

The Wilson murder became, then, another tragic accident. When Marty Albinder got out of the hospital and went around telling anybody who would listen that his wife shooting him had been a tragic accident, everybody, including, ultimately, the police, was happy to accept that explanation. First of all, he was a Yankee from Brooklyn, and besides, he was still alive—and still married to the alleged perpetrator. Jean Harris, the former headmistress of the Madeira School, tried the "tragic accident" defense with considerably less success when she shot her lover, the Scarsdale Diet doctor, Herman Tarnower. Harris told police that she had gone to his house to kill herself, but that when Tarnower tried to get the gun out of her hands, it went off and killed him instead. The problem was that ballistics experts testified that the shots were fired from something like seven feet away while the man was still lying in his bed. Harris served fifteen years of her sentence before being granted parole. She should have had Sonny Meridith as her lawyer. When I told Meridith I had never had an accident with as many guns as Oltremari used on Marty, he looked at me with a totally straight face and said, "It wasn't but two."

Jean Harris's biggest problem was that her trial was in White Plains, New York. Also, instead of a crucifix she wore a mink coat and an attitude and made way too much of her innocence and her integrity instead of the fact that she had been sorely mistreated by a two-timer who had gotten her hooked on diet pills. "Do you think," I asked my father, "Jean Harris would have gotten off if she had been in Mississippi?"

"Oh, hell yes," he said. "That cat sounded like a very bad guy."

American Beauty

When we are young our hairstyles are dictated by our mothers. My own mother used to pull the hair around my face straight back into a barrette or rubber band, a hairstyle that remains supremely unflattering to my long face, and which I hated. Mothers are always doing horrible things to their children's hair, their constantly repeated aim being to "get your hair out of your eyes," a goal that I think is maternal and universal and doesn't have a thing to do with where you live. It is only later, when your world gets bigger than your mother's bathroom, that your hair falls prey to outside forces: the girls at school, but mostly those on the cheerleading squad or in the homecoming court; the local salon (ours was Styles by Sarah), where they always have pictures of different hairstyles on the wall but nobody ever chooses them and all the clients look exactly the same; the select few women in the Junior League or in the Garden Club who give the most talked-about cocktail parties and wear the most stylish clothes. Our hair succumbs, in other words, to the ruling culture of where we live.

I lived in Mississippi, a place that once produced Miss America two years in a row, so that when I was growing up everybody wanted to have hair like Mary Ann Mobley, the winner in 1959, who made her way to Hollywood and married Gary Collins; or Bobbie Gentry, the very sexy country singer from Chickasaw County whose big hit was "Ode to Billy Joe." They looked a lot alike, actually, with long brown hair piled up high on top and long bangs that swept across the face to one side. There are still women in my hometown who look like this. I can think of one in particular who is still trying to maintain her beauty-queen image—and all that long, piled-up hair—against increasing odds.

Anyway, there is no question that where you're from dictates your hairdo, a fact driven home to me the other day when I was in the Dallas airport and I saw a woman with dyed-blond hair, all one color and sort of windswept, but only if the wind had stopped in midgust and her hair had been caught, sprayed in place, and frozen in time. I knew she was from Dallas because she worked in the airport, but she couldn't have been from anywhere else with that impenetrable blond hair helmet, just as Virginia Kelly, Bill Clinton's late mother, could not have been from, say, Oregon, with that white skunk stripe running through her shoe-polish-black teased-up hair.

To prove my theory, *Vogue* sent a gorgeous German model,

Georgia Goettmann, the winner of the 1994 Ford's Super-model of the World contest; an equally gorgeous fashion editor, Anne Christensen; and me to four American cities. We had Georgia done up in Minneapolis, New York, Palm Beach, and Memphis. And we came back with hard evidence that regionalism is still alive and kicking in America.

In Minneapolis, Georgia's look was clean. Minnesota, after all, is the home of Hazelden and a lot of other treatment centers like it where people come to dry out and get straight, and when it works, a lot of people decide to stay where they are, in the land of clean living. I know this because my sister-in-law grew up just outside Minneapolis. She is gorgeous and funny and we love her, but I still don't think her family, good Lutherans all, have gotten over us. They are nice people, healthy; they don't drink a lot of whiskey or dye their hair or smoke cigarettes. They don't like chemicals of any kind. My sister-in-law's grandmother slept with the windows open in her apartment one entire winter (Minnesota has subzero temperatures in winter—her husband slept with his earmuffs on) because she said the new carpet she bought smelled like it might have been treated with something strange.

The Minneapolis stylists making Georgia over followed this ethos. Her hair was washed in an all-natural product called Shampure, it was styled with only four big rollers for a "simple" look, her makeup was done in earth tones with names like "moon" and "sand." In New York, wholesome simplicity was replaced with severity and Georgia looked like a model again. Her eye makeup was graphic, her lips red, and her nails almost black. Her hair was ramrod straight and sexy, courtesy of the impossible-to-get-into Garren; her spike heels were by Manolo Blahnik. Georgia, who had been extremely pouty up to this point, was actually happy. And then, when we got to Palm Beach, severity was replaced with sheer size.

"Tanned, blond, big hair," says Margrit, owner of Salon Margrit, where pretty much everybody in Palm Beach comes to get their hair and makeup done. "It's the look." She gives it to Georgia, complete with a bronzer, fat blond streaks, and one of the wavy blond hairpieces in the salon's vast collection. Georgia was already blond, but it was low-key and natural-looking, and in Palm Beach, land of full-blown ball gowns, multiple face-lifts, and huge jewels, looking natural is not necessarily the goal. If you streak your hair, you want people to know it. And you need the extra help of the hairpiece because your real hair could not possibly stand up to the pressure of all the many events where it must do its duty. During the season, there are more than one hundred registered charity functions that the ladies feel obliged to attend, and that doesn't begin to count the endless fashion shows, gallery openings, and bridge breakfasts. Or the separate balls to honor the ladies who put on the charity balls. There is even a Croquet Ball, at the venerable Breakers Hotel, so we take Georgia there to play a game on the hotel court. When we get there, it's almost disappointing—no one even slows down to look. Margrit has done her job. Georgia looks like every other pretty Palm Beach party girl.

When we get to Memphis, everybody looks. We're at baggage claim at the airport and Georgia has on boots, tight jeans, and a tight sweater. She's wiped off her tan, her hairpiece is long gone, and her hair is pulled back into a ponytail that she plays with, bored. She has to be a model—Memphis girls don't look this way. A half dozen grown men stand together and undress her with their eyes, talking low to each other out of the sides of their mouths. I shoot them a stern look. They know I know they're out of their league, but finally, as we're leaving, they give it a try: "Are you here for a shoot?" It was touching, really—good ole boys trying hard to get the lingo down.

They don't know how to handle a girl like this. They can handle waitresses who call them "darlin'," their secretaries, their wives, and their girlfriends. They are not daunted by beauty queens or what passes for Memphis royalty, the Queen of the Cotton Carnival and her maids, because those women are soft, accessible, all gold and pink, like Linda Thompson, Elvis's girlfriend who once represented Tennessee in the Miss USA pageant. Memphis girls don't wear a lot of black and they wouldn't be caught dead in public without their makeup. They are Southern belles (who, as we all know, are tough as nails and hold the real power in the territory below the Mason-Dixon line) and they prefer to look soft. They know it is far more effective to look like the magnolia and not the steel. This philosophy is very much in evidence at the aptly named Diva Colour Studio, where we all go at the crack of dawn because they are too busy to work us in any other time. Diva is where everybody in the vicinity comes to get their hair done. They come from Arkansas and the Mississippi Delta and, of course, from all over Memphis, to see Roy.

"No matter what I say," he says, "you will hear me end

with the word 'soft.' " He calls Georgia's obvious Palm Beach highlights a "tragic mistake," and I don't tell him that in Palm Beach those big fat stripes are not a tragedy but an art form.

While Roy works his magic on Georgia, mixing up no less than nine different shades of blond, the makeup artist, Lee, leans his head over to show me his hair, also colored by Roy. "Touch it," he says. "Isn't it soft?" It is, actually, and so is Georgia's when Roy is done, very blond but somehow subtle, like the makeup Lee applies to her face. "When I do lessons, I have clients bring their own makeup, and I try to eliminate all the blues and greens. Memphis women still have a habit of painting their eyes to match their clothes." On Georgia's eyes, he puts "maize" and "almond," and pale pink on her cheeks and lips to match her freshly painted nails. "The hotter it gets, honey, the pinker I'll go," Lee says. Roy adjusts his color for the season as well. "Starting about February or March, I start lightening it up, so by the time you hit high June it's blond."

By that clock Georgia has definitely hit high June, maybe even July, but she looks great—she could easily pass for a Maid of Cotton, or chairman of rush week at the Ole Miss Chi Omega house. She has lots of loose curls that are casually pulled up off her face. Roy says he won't do updos anymore, that the most he'll go for, even at night, is a French twist. "If you have a gorgeous gown, nothing detracts from it more than a big hairdo."

Just hours later, his last pronouncement proves to be true. We are at lunch at the heavenly Four Way Grill on Mississippi Avenue, profoundly grateful to be eating some of the best fried chicken and cornbread muffins in America, served by a very amused Miss Dot, who has never seen a person as skinny as Georgia eat so much. But there she is, munching on big bowls of turnip greens and mashed potatoes with her glowing pink-tinged face and new soft blond hair, and the only thing the ladies at the next table can talk about is her dress, a full-skirted, red-and-white-checked DKNY. "Oh Lord, I haven't seen one of those in years," says one, referring to the crinoline underneath. "I used to love to wear a dress like that every Easter." "The skirt comes up when you sit down, you know," says the other. "I know, but I hear those dresses are coming back." Finally, the discussion comes round to Georgia herself. "She sure is pretty," they both say in unison. Yes, she is, and very, very soft.

Southern Fashion Explained

A few $years$ ago I wrote a story for *Vogue* in which I made the point that where you come from dictates the style of your hair. To prove it, a fashion editor and I dragged a German model named Georgia to four cities around the country and had the locals in each place do her hair and makeup, and then we dressed her up and took her out and photographed the results.

It's the kind of story I like. It's not rocket science and it doesn't take long. It even worked. Georgia's makeover in each spot proved that regional character endures despite tiresome theories to the contrary. In Palm Beach, she looked like a tanned blond socialite. In Minneapolis, she was clean and wholesome. In Manhattan, she was trendy and severe, with sixties hair and bloodred lips. But it was in Memphis that everybody said she looked the best: all soft and pink and gold-tinged, dressed in high, high heels and the full-skirted dresses of the season, her curls pulled up loosely off her face. And it was Memphis that got me in trouble.

We were in the airport, having just arrived, late, from Palm Beach. Georgia was sleepy and grumpy and she had on what almost every model in the world wears between shoots: a ratty black sweater and tight black jeans with boots and a black leather coat. All her Palm Beach bronze makeup had been wiped off, and her hair was pulled back in a messy pony-tail. There was not a man in the place who knew what to make of this sullen, unmade-up, but still gorgeous Amazon. Jaws dropped, sides were nudged, half-assed attempts to approach her were made. In the end, they couldn't do it. These boys were out of their league. Memphis girls, I wrote, don't look this way.

The fact is that very few people in airports anywhere look like ridiculously well paid, twenty-something German super-models. But the point I was making was that no self-respecting Memphis girl would be caught dead in an airport, about the most public of places after all, in wrinkled clothes and un-brushed hair, without makeup or jewelry, no matter how good-looking she might be. Especially not in the Memphis airport. Every single person who lives in the Mid-South who is going anywhere must change planes in Memphis. You are bound to see someone you know. When I said Memphis girls don't look that way, I meant they wouldn't dare.

I once saw three Chi Omegas jogging on the Ole Miss campus at seven-thirty in the morning in pale pink sweatsuits, full makeup, and perky ponytails tied with matching pink bows. (A friend of mine calls this particular type of Southern girl a "bowhead.") If they exercise in eye makeup and lipstick, they certainly aren't going to the airport in anything less. But all this was lost on the *Vogue* readers who reside below the Mason-Dixon line. They barraged me with hate mail and accused me of insulting the whole of Southern womanhood. The letters all said the same things: How dare you insinuate that we are plain in comparison to a German model? We are as stylish and beautiful and sophisticated as any woman anywhere, and most important, we are sick to death of Yankees coming down here and making fun of us. (They had missed the part where I presented my credentials as a non-Yankee, where I said that I grew up in Greenville, Mississippi, and that all the women there wanted big, long hair like Bobbie Gentry and our most popular Miss Mississippi, Mary Ann Mobley.) "From now on," one particularly riled-up woman from South Carolina wrote, "stay in New York where you belong and don't come down here anymore."

The letter writers were exhibiting the deep-dyed fear that lives in the heart of every Southerner, myself included: that a Yankee is putting us down. This enormous chip we carry on our shoulders makes us defensive, scared, and sometimes stupid. First of all, these women should have been thrilled that they don't look like New Yorkers, or, for that matter, Germans. I just spent three days on a Russian train with some German feminists who were bound for the United Nations' Conference on Women in Beijing, and I guarantee you that nobody in her right mind would aspire to look the way they looked, with their crew-cut hairdos and rat-tail braids at the napes of their necks, their drab tunics and Birkenstocks. And to dress like a committed New Yorker often means losing your individuality. I can tell you what every woman in New York will be dressing like in six months by looking at what the very tall and beautiful young *Vogue* fashion assistants are wearing to the office. People dress in packs in New York. Just as Southerners are terrified of being looked down on, New Yorkers are terrified of not being up to the minute. Every Sunday in the Style section of *The New York Times* there is a photographic feature of several different women all in the same "look." A photographer stands on the street and snaps women who are wearing the same thing. That's it. So there might be five pictures of five women in the same Chanel suit with a hat that was the hit of the spring shows, or seven pictures of seven women in trench coats with Prada handbags. Every fashion-obsessed woman of means in New York who does not carry an Hermès Kelly bag carries a black nylon Prada handbag from Italy. No right-thinking Southern person would dream of paying $1,000 for a nylon tote that you could buy for $15 at Wal-Mart or Target, except for the fact that it has a tiny metal triangle affixed to it that bears the word "Prada." New York women live for that triangle. This is not something you should aspire to. And why in the world would you worry what people so neurotic and style-conscious think of you?

We can't help it. Every Southerner alive, at many, many points in their childhood, heard the words, "But what will people think?" It was usually uttered before one of the children in question was about to commit some horrible social crime like wearing a tie-dyed T-shirt. My own father once told me I could never again wear the jeans I had just worn to eat lunch at Sherman's Grocery Store because they had holes in the knees—holes I had carefully cultivated, holes I prayed would hurry up and appear. It was a grocery store, for God's sake, where you stood in line and ordered plate lunches and barbecue sandwiches, but everybody in town ate lunch there, and there was just no telling what they might think.

When the novelist Peter Taylor died in 1994, Shelby Foote told National Public Radio that what Taylor had done better than anybody else was to illustrate the Southerner's obsession with appearances, our acute consciousness of the impression we make on other people. Keeping up appearances—the appearance of wealth, the appearance of breeding, the appearance of piety—is a particularly Southern art form. Some people would rather go hungry than sell the family silver or the family portraits or give up the membership to the country club. We may have lost everything, but we don't want anybody, especially any Yankees, to know it. And if all else fails, we've still got our dignity—or, more accurately, our sense of propriety. My grandmother chain-smoked Pall Malls, but she would've had a nicotine fit before she would smoke on the street. When she traveled, she dressed like a queen, a practice still upheld by a great many of the women who navigate the endless hallways of the Memphis airport, though not by self-absorbed models unencumbered by fears of what the men and women of the South might think.

The most entertaining encounter I ever had in the Memphis airport was with someone I had gone to school with in the Delta. I was in my twenties and hadn't seen this guy since tenth grade. He was a deckhand and very drunk, and on his way to St. Louis to catch a towboat. When I recognized him, I remembered how sweet he'd been. He recognized me too and came over and said, with utter seriousness, that he just wanted me to know that he had never, ever believed my best friend Jessica and I had been dykes, no matter what anybody had said. He was referring to our rebellious period during which we wore huaraches with jeans and T-shirts or gauze "hippie" blouses to school in defiance of the dress code at the white racist academy we attended. Every other girl's aspiration was to be elected class beauty or "cutest" or homecoming queen and she would have died before putting on flat (ugly) shoes or shapeless shirts. "I always thought y'all were cool," he said, standing there at least a decade after we'd last seen each other, and I think I may have kissed him.

On Saturdays, in good weather, the girls who went to our school put on makeup and their boyfriends' football jerseys and rode around all day in somebody's convertible with their hair rolled up in huge pink rollers and sometimes in empty frozen orange juice cans. The whole exercise was designed to let people know that they had dates that night. In this one instance, the rollers weren't considered tacky. They were an acceptable accessory, a badge that proclaimed the wearer was the most coveted of all things: She was popular. It was an elaborate ritual, but then most things in this part of the country are. For women in the South, clothes, jewelry, the way they wear their hair or do their makeup, even their giant pink rollers, are part of a larger arsenal of feminine wiles. They are the weapons of flirtation and glamour, of power, class warfare, intimidation, and seduction. There's more to getting dressed here than putting on an Armani suit and feeling fashion-safe and presentable. I once saw a photograph in a magazine of a Memphis woman I know, dressed to the teeth and lying on a tanning bed—in her closet—surrounded by clothes and shoes and scarves and jewelry and belts and gloves. That closet reminded me of a war room.

Of course, the finished product is full of nuances.

Georgia acquired a girlish, pink femininity in Memphis, a Maid-of-Cotton effect. Had we taken her to a salon along the Southeastern seaboard, she would have been given a more ladylike sheen. When I finally threw a fit and left the white racist academy (the principal, who also happened to be the football coach, had called me into his office for reading a book during a pep rally, and that was the last straw), I discovered the girls of the Carolinas. I was at an all-girls boarding school in Virginia, right outside of Washington. It was probably the hardest I've ever worked in my life. Since I preferred to get some much-needed sleep during the ten or fifteen minutes it would have taken me to properly dress, I went to class every day with my flannel nightgown tucked into my jeans and an alarmingly unattractive ski jacket that had the stuffing coming out of it. At dinner most of us would meet the requirement that we wear a skirt by wrapping our gym kilts over what we already had on. Not the Carolina girls. They were appalled by our behavior. They wore real skirts, wraparound ones from the Talbot's catalog, in madras patchwork or cotton with appliquéd ladybugs in the spring, and tartan or gray flannel in the winter. They wore gold add-a-bead necklaces and clip-on earrings to class (they would never have done anything so common as pierce their ears), their hair was held back by velvet-covered headbands or gold barrettes, and their turtlenecks had rosebuds embroidered on them. Even their jeans were corduroy. My roommate was from Wadesboro, North Carolina, and I will never forget the expression on her mother's face when she walked in and saw me for the first time, on that first day, dressed in the vestiges of my rebel period: jeans, Adidas T-shirt, and Earth shoes. She was carrying a box of African violets (naturally) to put on our windowsill and she almost dropped them.

I grew up in the Mississippi Delta, where we are neither pink nor pulled-together and ladylike. Girls are taught to drink scotch and smoke cigarettes and drive a car by the time they are twelve. When I was four years old I was given my first lesson on how to do the twist, and I spent most weekend afternoons in our pear tree observing the bad behavior of my parents and their friends at the wild parties of my next-door neighbors. The women always looked incredibly sophisticated in silk pajamas and linen shifts and the men wore linen too, or seersucker. My favorite game was dress-up, but only if I could wear my mother's black cocktail dresses, which I would rig up, somehow, to fit me. I dressed up at boarding school too, but I saved my energy for weekends, when we might see some actual men, and then I'd lend my friends my adult-looking Delta clothes, bought at Hafter's Department Store, and the jewelry my grandmother had given me, and we'd all go into town and try to restore some lost dignity to our otherwise overworked and extremely grubby existence.

The thing all of us, from the Carolinas to the Delta, have in common is the desire to look like women in every sense of the word. (During that brief period when I didn't, after all, the whole high school thought I was dating my best friend.) We were all taught to enhance what God gave us—there is not a lot of hiding our lights under a bushel down here. The grunge look of the early nineties never took off in a big way in the South, and there are not a lot of women taking cover under Issey Miyake's bat-wing raincoats or Yohji Yamamoto's boxy suits. Once, after I had spent about two months' salary on some up-to-the-minute gray-and-white Yamamoto chopped pants and matching oversize tunic, my grandfather refused to take me to Nashville's Belle Meade Country Club in them, on the grounds that I looked like I had on my nightclothes. Even in her old age, my grandmother had worn longline bras to keep her shape, and my grandfather could not imagine why any woman would want to dress the way I had.

A colleague of mine at *Vogue* once did a story in which she traveled around the country showing slides—runway shots—of the spring collections of various designers. The women of Chicago and San Francisco loved the Armani pantsuits, the simple Calvin Klein evening gowns like slips, the unadorned Ralph Lauren dresses with matching jackets. They didn't have much to say about the clothes, really, and in the article, those women got two paragraphs. The women of Houston and Atlanta, on the other hand, had a whole lot to say about what they looked at, and they got three times the space. The first thing they couldn't get over was that none of the clothes was shown with jewelry and accessories. The look that particular season was spare and streamlined but they didn't care. "We sleep in earrings in the South," a woman from Atlanta told the writer. A woman from Houston repeated the memorable line from *Steel Magnolias*, informing her that "what separates us from the beasts is our ability to accessorize." The women from Atlanta, close to their Carolina sisters, said they would only wear the Armani suits that were shown with pretty gathered skirts. ("My husband wouldn't like it if I wore pants at night," one said.) They also held fast to the still-strict codes of Southern dressing, a discussion sparked by John Galliano, who had shown his forties suits, very chicly, actually, with black tights and white patent-leather, spike-heeled Mary Janes. Now I love Galliano, and the *Vogue* assistants that year had been running around in the black-tights-and-white-patent combo for so long that I had ceased to notice it anymore. I'd forgotten what the women of Atlanta were adamant about: that to wear white shoes of any kind after Labor Day and before Easter is an unpardonable sin. It is, as usual, a matter of what people would think if they wore them. You can't even wear black patent leather unless it's summer, they said, and white patent on grown women, especially with black stockings, is so trashy it doesn't deserve discussion. In addition, you are not supposed to wear white to a wedding (it will upstage the bride) or black—anywhere—until after Labor Day.

In the *Vogue* survey, the women of Houston especially hated black. They loved the Chanel suits, but only in red, and they loved Armani, but in orange. They loved the Galliano ball gowns with tight canary-yellow bodices and huge tulle skirts, and they really loved the fur. "Fake fur is so unwonderful," the Reveillon fur manager at the Houston Saks told me once, as he tried mightily to sell me a chinchilla stole I could not remotely afford. This man does an astounding amount of business, despite the fact that no one in Houston actually needs a fur coat to keep warm.

But warmth is not the reason the women of Houston wear fur coats. They wear them for the same reason they still wear ball gowns made of tulle, to get attention, to stop a room. In addition to keeping up appearances, Southern women are raised to make entrances. I have a very curvy friend who grew up in both Atlanta and Charleston, and I asked her the other day what possessed her to go through a long period after college in which she wore almost nothing at night but skintight dresses covered in sequins or bugle beads or both. She didn't miss a beat. "For impact. For the sense that all eyes are on you, that the whole room has frozen." Now this woman has a Ph.D. in theology, but I realized when she said that, that there are women all over the South who were taught to think about how their clothes would catch the light no matter what their occupation. This is in part because every city and every town is blessed with a pageant lady, one of those women who gets her hands on girls early, and who steers them—with their mothers' blessings—from Miss Toddler Hospitality all the way to Atlantic City if they're lucky. We have one at home. She takes them in and teaches them how to carry themselves and what to say, how to hone talent when there is none, how to glide along in those sparkly dresses that dazzle the TV cameras and make large parts of the American South look like Hollywood on Oscar night.

When I was growing up, I was always told that Mississippi had more Miss Americas than any other state, a fact I found out was wrong when I tried to put it in *Vogue* and a zealous fact checker wouldn't let me. It doesn't matter—we have plenty of other "titled women," as my father has always insisted on calling the legions of beauty queens who clutter the landscape.

Once, before I was born, Greenville was the site of the annual convention of the American Waterways Organization, a group of barge and towboat operators from around the country. Some of the organization's members, including my father, were having a drink at the extremely inaccurately named Yacht Club (annual dues, $10; yachts, none), where they met a girl from across the river who listed among her titles Queen of the Turtle Derby, Miss Pink Tomato, and second runner-up to Miss Arkansas. When she told them about her titles, they decided that the convention could not continue without a Queen of the Waterways. Like the good pageant girl she was, she protested that she couldn't be crowned without a contest, as it wouldn't be fair to all the other girls who might want to have the chance to reign over the nation's rivers. But they assured her that she would win the contest anyway, and that it was only lack of a crown that presented a problem, whereupon she announced that she had one with her, in her suitcase in her room at the Downtowner Motor Inn. So they got some ribbon from the florist and wrote "Queen of the Waterways" on it in glitter, and her picture was on the front page of the *Delta Democrat-Times* with Jesse Brent, legendary towboat operator and that year's president of the AWO.

Now that story has been told to me at least a dozen times but I never tire of hearing it because I am still blown away by the fact that that girl traveled with her crown. There is a pride and resourcefulness in this idiotic child-woman that speaks to me. And there is a graciousness too. Georgia, standing there pouting in the Memphis airport, thought that beauty was everything and effort unnecessary. Southern women know better. The Queen of the Turtle Derby and her crown prove to me one all-consuming fact: More than anything, more than we are obsessed with appearances, more than we like to look soft or ladylike, more than we want to stop a room or win a man or an argument or a seat at the table with what we are wearing, Southern women know how to rise to the occasion.

Cat Fight

I should declare my loyalty to catfish upfront. Or, more precisely, to American farm-raised catfish, more than 70 percent of which comes from the Mississippi Delta, where I grew up.

During my brief career as a business reporter, I wrote about the fledgling catfish industry first for the *Orlando Sentinel* and then for *U.S. News & World Report*. The Catfish Farmers of America were so grateful that they sent me a plaque "in recognition for the contribution made . . . through the use of [my] craft." More thrillingly, they asked me to reign as a sort of ad hoc Catfish Queen and ride on their float in the 1987 Mobile, Alabama, Mardi Gras parade with Jerry Clower. I wouldn't accept because I didn't feel that I had earned my title in the proper manner (and I probably was too embarrassed). But now the fact that I didn't remains one of my greatest regrets. I assume I would have gotten to wear a crown, and I have always imagined that it would have been in the shape of two catfish with their mouths meeting in the middle, their rhinestone whiskers shimmering above my forehead.

Mississippi is as famous for its beauty queens—who represent everything from towns and schools to agricultural products—as it is for its catfish. We have so many that "to queen" is actually a verb. The whole state has been in a Miss America frenzy since Mary Ann Mobley and Lynda Lee Mead won back-to-back titles in 1959 and 1960. In the years between 1980 and 1990, we had more consecutive swimsuit winners (women do not wear "bathing suits" in the Miss America pageant) than any other state, a record that still stands. In 1996, the first time viewers were allowed to phone in their votes, I called everybody I know and begged them to turn on their television sets and vote for Miss Mississippi, who should, of course, have won.

Also, for every Catfish Queen and Poultry Princess, there is a Little Miss Catfish Queen and Baby Miss Poultry Princess; for every Miss Northside Mall, there is a Tiny Miss Northside Mall.

Since I had not been queening from birth on, the catfish title would have been my first and last shot. But I wasn't sure that I was up to the job. Aside from the embarrassment factor, I had no real connection with the catfish I would have been representing. It is—forgive me—a relatively new breed of cat, bearing almost no resemblance to the omnivorous, mud-loving bottom feeders my father and I fished for when I was little. While queening and fishing for catfish are time-honored pastimes (and in many cases vocations), raising catfish did not become a career choice until the late 1970s and '80s.

That was when Mississippi farmers faced the worst depression since the 1930s. Those who didn't want to give up the land altogether (and who, more importantly, could still get a bank loan) decided to trade in their soybean and cotton seeds for fish fingerlings and started digging ponds. Since then, the farmers and their trade organizations, the Catfish Farmers of America and the Catfish Institute, have spent at least $70 million aggressively marketing their product. They printed endless cookbooks (including my favorite, *Fishing for Compliments—Cooking with Catfish*), published impressive stats (the fish is raised in environmentally controlled conditions; it is low in fat and cholesterol), and supported enormous events like the Catfish Festival in Belzoni, Mississippi, a community of 2,660 that is rightly billed as the Catfish Capital of the World. Last year 630 million pounds of farm-raised catfish were processed in the United States, bringing an estimated $243 million to Mississippi alone, with an impact of more than $2 billion on the state's economy.

So when the Vietnamese started peddling catfish from the Mekong Delta in this country under brand names like Delta Select (a moniker mighty close to the popular Mississippi brand Delta Pride), the farmers got very upset. One of the first things the Americans challenged was the right of the Vietnamese farmers to use the word itself. They maintain that the Vietnamese fish is really basa fish, whatever that is, and that labeling it as catfish is, in the words of Hugh Warren, executive vice president of the CFA, the equivalent of "selling kangaroo meat as sirloin." Last year the CFA persuaded Congress to bar the Vietnamese from calling their fish catfish, and to require them to stamp their packages with the country of origin so there wouldn't be any more confusion about which delta had been the fish's birthplace.

Since there are more than two thousand species of catfish in the world, it does seem a tad ridiculous to contend that our North American family, *Ictaluridae,* is the only one that can be correctly called catfish. But in this current war with Vietnam, at least, I am firmly on our side. I can't help it. I have never been good at escaping my roots. And I honestly do believe it is a superior product.

Farm-raised catfish are pure little packages of protein, raised in ponds filled with aerated and circulated well water and fed pellets composed of soybeans and corn. They don't taste muddy; they taste sweet. John Egerton, the Southern historian and food writer who laments what has happened to the taste of chickens since they've been mass-produced, admits that farm-raised catfish are "an anomaly: one of the few artificially produced foods that may be better than the original." Nothing, he says, "beats pond-raised catfish, not even the native cats of the South's lakes and rivers."

The latter is a point the American catfish farmers have seized on in their battle with the Vietnamese, who raise their fish in huge underwater pens in the polluted Mekong River. "They've grown up flapping around in third-world rivers and dining on whatever they can get their fins on," read one advertisement produced by the catfish lobby. Representative Marion Berry of Arkansas, whose state is also a top catfish producer, went so far as to accuse the Vietnamese fish of being contaminated with Agent Orange. "That stuff doesn't break down." That last crack is a bit much, especially since we're the ones who sprayed the stuff over there in the first place. Also, now the farmers are claiming that the Vietnamese are illegally "dumping" their catfish on the U.S. market at artificially low prices, and they've asked the Commerce Department to impose import duties. The department responded with a preliminary ruling recommending import duties of as much as 64 percent. The Vietnamese contend that this violates the spirit of free trade and that the United States is protecting the interests of "a relatively small group of wealthy catfish industrialists."

I have to confess that I agree with the free trade part, but until now "wealthy" and "industrialist" were not words I thought I would ever live to see bracketing "catfish." First of all, these days you don't get rich (much less become a personage as impressive as an industrialist) farming anything in the Mississippi Delta. Also, catfish has always been an inexpensive food for the masses. At catfish fries across the South, hundreds and sometimes thousands are fed—the world's biggest, which serves 12,500 pounds of catfish, lasts about a week and is held every April in Paris, Tennessee. A staple of old-fashioned Southern retail politicking, a catfish fry features fillets dredged in seasoned cornmeal and deep-fried in huge drums of roiling oil, accompanied by tartar sauce, pickles, coleslaw, and fries.

I threw a catfish fry once, in my hometown, to celebrate the fiftieth birthday of a visiting British friend. In deference to our honored guest, some of the guests wore tiaras, one of which was made entirely of cotton bolls. When I saw it, I realized what an idiot I had been. The party would have been the perfect opportunity to have commissioned and worn the rhinestone catfish tiara I had envisioned. Which has given me an idea as to how I'll celebrate my own fiftieth. I'll have a catfish fry, of course, where I'll reign, at last, as Catfish Queen.

Whiskey Weather

$\mathcal{A}$ few years ago the New Orleans city government printed up bumper stickers designed to make the residents feel better about where they live: NEW ORLEANS, PROUD TO CALL IT HOME. They should have known better. No one could possibly have taken it seriously. Within days, a far more popular—and accurate—knockoff hit the streets: NEW OR-LEANS, PROUD TO CALL IT HELL.

Calling New Orleans home means living in a place that has almost as many murders as days of the year and a humidity level so high that it's hard to tell the air from the water. The mosquitoes are so bad there is a twenty-four-member Mosquito Control Board in charge of them, and we spend almost $40 million a year in an attempt to control the flying Formosan termites who are literally eating up the city. Caterpillars with toxic spines are chewing the leaves off our trees, and packs of feral hogs are destroying the levees that keep the place from flooding. Living here is not unlike living in the Old Testament.

The summer of the bumper stickers was the hottest in ninety years. On the first day of June it was 98 degrees Fahrenheit. In July an electrical transformer blew up on Bourbon Street and the French Quarter was without electricity for two days. In August it rained so hard the streets were under water for two days. So in September, it seemed inevitable that Hurricane Georges would be heading right at us.

As the world now knows, at the last minute the storm moved a few miles east and hit the Mississippi Gulf Coast instead, but we weren't immediately out of danger. Ten thousand alligators escaped from the world's largest alligator farm in Pascagoula, Mississippi, which is not much more than an hour down the road from here. Georges had given the gators their freedom, and only a very few were ever caught. Compared to this stuff, frogs in my kneading bowl would be the good news.

Living in the land of pestilence and plagues gives everyone an excuse to drink heavily. I was not actually in New Orleans for the Georges scare but I wished I had been. My lifelong friend McGee called me in New York about every twenty minutes to tell me what a great time she was having and that she could not believe I wasn't in town. "Girl, you are really missing it." She had holed up in her third-floor apartment with a twenty-eight-year-old Australian sailor, a gallon of bourbon, and a case of Cokes. My landlady bought a case of wine and a quart of gin. Terranova's grocery store opened up for a few hours so that people could stock up on supplies, and the first thing they ran out of was vermouth.

Every place in town ultimately closed except the Red Door bar, whose customers drank their whiskey wearing hard hats, and the Richelieu Hotel, which is conveniently located across the street from McGee. The staff didn't show up so McGee and assorted other regulars helped out, serving bacon and eggs and brandy milk punches all day. Had I been there I would have made everyone pitchers of Hurricanes, an excellent native concoction made of dark rum, light rum, lime juice, orange juice, pineapple juice, and mango syrup. Most people in their right mind, of course, left town. The last hurricane that actually hit New Orleans, Betsy, in 1965, killed more than a hundred people. But, as my landlady pointed out, her house was built in 1836 and it is still standing. I think she was disappointed that she didn't get to crack open the gin. "It was only a two-bottle-of-wine hurricane," she told me glumly.

A wine shop was in fact the first commercial establishment in the city and it is no wonder. A year after Bienville established New Orleans as the capital of Louisiana in 1718, a hurricane wiped out the handful of palmetto huts that had been erected after they cleared what remains essentially a swamp. An engineer named Le Blond de la Tour tried to tell Bienville to move New Orleans to a place that was not, for example, five inches below sea level, between the world's widest river and a pretty big lake, but he refused to budge. Two years later, four city blocks had been built when another hurricane came and knocked them out. Finally, they figured out that things might last longer if they were made out of bricks, which is why, despite many subsequent hurricanes, we are still stuck here today.

McGee and my landlady may be crazy, but they were not nearly as nuts as the thousands of people who piled inside the Superdome, the enormous enclosed stadium where the New Orleans Saints football team plays when they are home, and which served as the city's official shelter during the storm. It wasn't much of a shelter since you had to bring your own bedding and they ran out of food and water. People stood in line with their lawn chairs and coolers and boom boxes, thinking they might actually have some fun, until they got inside and discovered even fresher hell than usual. As you might expect in a city with our crime rate, there were all kinds of thefts and fights, and at one point a full-blown riot broke out.

Also, once you got in, you couldn't get out. National Guardsmen stood at every exit with rifles, blocking the many people who decided they would rather take their chances with Georges than stay inside an airless dome with a large segment of the city's criminal population. After two days, on Sunday, when it became clear that there was not going to be a hurricane after all, everybody got to go home. It had barely rained. Still, half the city's electricity was out for two more days, and schools, banks, and city offices remained closed for almost a week. There is a reason why we have another bumper sticker that is also extremely popular in these parts: LOUISIANA, THIRD WORLD AND PROUD OF IT.

On Soggy Ground

In 1960, when I was born, Mississippi had then been dry for fifty-two years. This, to me, remains an astonishing fact, particularly since I didn't learn it until 1972, six years after Prohibition had finally come to an end. I had always thought I was a pretty sophisticated kid—I could have told you, for example, the names of Lyndon Johnson's dogs or of Richard Nixon's entire cabinet. More to the point, I knew that a Gibson contained onions and a martini olives (or a twist) and that Johnny Mercer and Hoagy Carmichael had written "In the Cool, Cool, Cool of the Evening," the song by which my mother invariably sang me to sleep. But, until a state law required me to take a Mississippi history course in the seventh grade, I did not know about another state law that was on the books until 1966: "No whiskey for any purpose whatsoever could be shipped into the State and no person could have, control, or possess any whiskey whatsoever."

This seemed incredible. One of my earliest memories is of my father teaching me to make his martini, a service which I performed for years afterward and for which I was paid ten cents per drink. At five, my friend McGee began a larger enterprise when, frustrated by the slow sales at our neighborhood lemonade stand, she looked at her sister and me and asked, "Have you ever seen Mama or Daddy or any of their friends drink lemonade?" We had to agree that we had not. We had seen them drink old-fashioneds and scotch sours, gin and tonics, Bloody Marys, and whole rafts full of cold beer in the summer, but we had never seen them drink much of anything else except for coffee and that was always early in the morning. McGee promptly pulled her wagon up to the vast refrigerator in her parents' garage, unloaded the contents, and got rich selling cold Pabst Blue Ribbon for twenty cents a can to the many thirsty passersby on our country road.

No wonder I had never heard of the law, which itself was full of complications. The Mississippi state legislature, like those of several other Southern states, passed a statewide "bone dry law" in 1908, more than a decade before the federal government prohibited alcohol in the form of the Eighteenth Amendment to the Constitution on January 16, 1919. Mississippi was the first state in the union to ratify the amendment, an act which moved the governor to give a speech about the good results of the law that Mississippi had already enjoyed. "The civil, economic, and moral life of our people has been greatly benefited by this law," he said, adding that "sentiment is growing in favor of prohibition. It is true that we have a number of people who are breaking the law, either making or using liquor, but this does not meet the approval of the highest class of our citizens. . . . Our people practically unanimously will vote to make the whole world dry."

He was right about the voting part at least. After the passage of the Twenty-first Amendment, which repealed the Eighteenth Amendment and officially ended federal prohibition on December 5, 1933, every other Southern state abandoned statewide prohibition except Mississippi, prompting the humorist Will Rogers to comment that Mississippians will continue to "vote dry as long as they can stagger to the polls." (To this day the legislature has not formally ratified the Twenty-first Amendment.) However, by 1944, the number of people willing to risk the disapproval of "the highest class of citizens" by "making or using liquor" had grown sufficiently that the state decided to tax the sale of alcohol even though it was still illegal. This new law did not ever actually mention the word "liquor." Rather, it called for a 10 percent sales tax on "tangible personal property, the sale of which is prohibited by law"—a bit of obfuscation that added up to $4.25 per case of whiskey, gin, etc., and seventy-five cents per gallon of wine.

By 1950, Mississippi had more retail liquor dealers, otherwise known as bootleggers, than any of the twenty-two legally wet states at the time, and more than twice the number in the two adjacent states of Tennessee and Arkansas combined. Furthermore, because booze was cheaper and more plentiful in Mississippi, the residents of Alabama and Georgia (both legally wet) drove over to buy their whiskey from us. In this free-flowing environment, law enforcement officers were generally well paid to look the other way, keeping up only half-hearted appearances for the sake of those few zealots among us. In 1952, for example, when my father's friend J.B. came to visit him from Memphis, he thoughtfully brought along a case of gin as a house present. After a long night of drinking at a popular local "tonk" owned by Mr. Paul E. "Mink" Maucelli, one of our more prominent bootleggers, J.B. got lost trying to follow my father home and was arrested—not for driving drunk, though he was, but because a cop mistook him for a robber in the neighborhood. J.B. was released but the gin was not, a breach of hospitality that caused considerable local outrage. When my father confronted the police chief about it at the station the next day, the chief, with some sadness, explained that he had no choice: "It wasn't just a bottle or two, Clarke, it was a whole case. A case. Why'd he have to drive around with a whole case in his car?" (At the cotton brokerage office next door, interest centered on the brand of the confiscated gin. "What kind was it?" asked one of the local characters, licking his lips. "Gordon's or Gilbey's?")

In 1965, state records show that more than 450,000 cases of whiskey and 150,000 cases of wine were taxed, figures that don't take into account the locally produced moonshine that constituted about 50 percent of the liquor market all through Prohibition. (It should be noted that the entire population of Mississippi is only two million.) Clearly, the people had found a way to live with the dry laws. As *The Wall Street Journal* noted six months before Prohibition was repealed, "Mississippi has arrived at a convenient and profitable arrangement with its conscience. The drys have their law, the wets have their liquor and the state has its taxes. Everybody's happy."

During the annual liquor-bill debate in the state legislature in 1952, Representative N. S. "Soggy" Sweat crystallized his colleagues' courageous stand on the issue in his famous "Whiskey Speech": "You ask me how I feel about liquor. Here's where I stand on this burning question. If when you say whiskey you mean the devil's brew, the poison scourge that defiles innocence, dethrones reason, destroys the home, creates misery and poverty, yea literally takes the bread from the mouths of little children; if you mean that evil concoction that topples the Christian man and woman from the pinnacles of gracious living down into the bottomless pit of degradation and despair, then certainly I am against it. But . . . if when you say whiskey you mean the oil of conversation, the philosophic wine, the ale that is consumed when good fellows get together, that puts a song in their hearts and laughter on their lips, and the warm glow of contentment in their eyes; if you mean Christmas cheer; if you mean the drink that enables a man to magnify his joy and his happiness, and to forget, if only for a little while, life's great tragedies, and heartaches, and sorrows; if you mean that drink which pours into our treasuries untold millions of dollars, which are used to provide tender care for our little crippled children, our blind, our deaf, our dumb, our pitiful aged and infirm; to build highways and hospitals and schools, then certainly I am for it. This is my stand. I will not retreat from it. I will not compromise."

The Real First Lady

Given the fact that Tammy Wynette was married five times (the fourth for less than two months) it is ironic that the title of her most famous song is "Stand by Your Man." She cowrote it, but it wasn't one of her favorites—she told a reporter that she "had no faith in that song" as a hit. It became one, of course, and went on to achieve cult status—appropriated by gay men as a camp anthem (it blares from the sound system of the bar down the street from my New Orleans house at least once every night), and by feminists who offer up its chorus as proof that women are still held back by weakness and desire. Most famously, it was employed by Hillary Clinton as a—sort of—defense against allegations that her husband had cheated on her with Gennifer Flowers. "I'm not sitting here," she told *60 Minutes* reporter Steve Kroft, "like some little woman standing by my man like Tammy Wynette."

Like the feminists, Hillary, who grew up in Illinois and probably didn't listen to a lot of Tammy or Loretta or anybody else, missed the point. The lyrics of "Stand by Your Man" echo a recurring theme in country music, that of the moral superiority of women, who stand by their lovers not because they're hopelessly enthralled, but because they know the boys can't help it. "After all," as the song says, "he's just a man." Since "he's only human" was a mantra of sorts in her husband's first campaign (George Stephanopoulos actually uttered that line to me on more than one occasion), Hillary should have known better. Also, one could argue that since that 1991 interview, she has come to embody the true meaning of the song, taking the high ground as it were, during many, many more of her husband's especially human moments.

The same could not be said for Tammy, whose subsequent hits included "D-I-V-O-R-C-E" and "Your Good Girl's Gonna Go Bad." True, she stuck it out with George Jones for a remarkable six years, and she'd been married to George Richey for twenty before she died, but, generally speaking, when the time came, she always knew when to get up and go. Now, five years after her death, she's getting ready to do it again.

As I write, Tammy is buried in a modest crypt in Woodlawn Memorial Park, but she won't be there too much longer if George Jones and his current wife, Nancy, have their way. Jones cannot get over the fact that, as he puts it, "she doesn't even know anybody over there where she is." Nancy reports that when she went to visit, gnats were everywhere, the place smelled bad, and there was only "one little bitty rose in a little bitty vase." She broke down and cried right there. "I was so upset. I said, 'This is awful. The First Lady of Country Music and she's buried in a damn wall.' "

The sorry state of Tammy's final resting place inspired George and Nancy to set about raising $106,000 so that she can be resituated in a proper crypt, one that will also have room for Tammy's four children and Richey. The plan is, in fact, for Tammy to be at George Jones's feet. "People are gonna say, 'See, he still loves her,' " says Nancy, but she doesn't care. "It'll be great for the fans" (who will have, in the words of Evelyn Shriver, the co-owner of Jones's record company, a "one-stop shop"). Tammy's first-ever publicity photo will be etched in a marble plaque on the ground, in between two benches flanking her crypt. George and Nancy's own crypt will be just above hers with their faces etched on either side of the doors, along with two giant guitars. Their own plaque will be inscribed with Jones's nickname, Possum.

All this will be on the grounds of the George Jones Estate at Woodlawn Cemetery in Franklin, Tennessee, a family plot that took on greater dimensions when Jones read in the paper that Johnny Paycheck, author and singer of the immortal "Take This Job and Shove It," died without enough money to have a decent burial. Nancy swung into action, got Paycheck buried in one of their plots, and arranged to buy a total of eighty-five—for other needy or deserving country stars, for Jones family members and close business associates, and, of course, for Tammy.

"I'm not doing it for publicity," Nancy says. "I'm too damn old and I don't need it." It's just that at Tammy's funeral she was appalled at the slapdash nature of it all. "We were standing there and I said to George, 'Lemme tell you what I want.' I come from the days when you plan this stuff, you pay for it, you know what you're going to wear." She laughs. "I'm burying my own self right."

It is fitting that Tammy will be buried with the two of her five husbands she stayed married to the longest: Jones, with whom she did some of her best work, notably the duets "(We're Not) The Jet Set" and "Two Story House"; and Richey, who cowrote the amazing " 'Til I Can Make It on My Own," inspired, as it happens, by her relationship with Jones. It's complicated. Tammy's life was complicated, so it's nice to think of her finally having a bit of peace.

Tammy Wynette was born Virginia Wynette Pugh in Itawamba County, Mississippi, in 1942. She left her first husband, Euple Byrd, when she was twenty-two, after five years of living in a log cabin with no stove or refrigerator or running water. She had three children (she was kicked out of high school for being pregnant with the first one), and when she put them in the car to head for Nashville and a career in country music, Euple laughed and told her to "dream on, baby, dream on." Which irritated Tammy. "Don't tell me that I can't do something," she said, " 'cause I'll show you I can."

She left her second husband, motel desk clerk and failed songwriter Don Chapel, after Jones, already her singing partner, interrupted an argument between them, kicked over the dining room table, and declared his love for her. She got in the car again, this time with Jones and the kids, and they drove all night to Georgia. When their marriage finally fell apart, Tammy generously took half the blame, attributing it to "his nippin' and my naggin'," but there had been plenty to nag about. In addition to serial bouts with booze, cocaine, and women, Jones had a penchant for guns. When his friend, the songwriter Earl "Peanutt" Montgomery, found the Lord and quit drinking and urged Jones to do the same, Jones pulled out a .38, said, "See if your God can save you now," and fired. He missed, but barely. One night, after he shot up his and Tammy's Lakeland, Florida, mansion with a rifle, he aimed it at her, according to her autobiography. According to his, he didn't, but either way, the police arrived and hauled him off in a straitjacket.

A year after her divorce from Jones, Tammy married Nashville Realtor Michael Tomlin and divorced him forty-four days later. She then had an affair with Burt Reynolds, whom she saved from drowning in her bathtub, before finally settling down with Richey.

After the Clintons' *60 Minutes* interview was aired, Tammy was mad as a hornet and declared that Hillary Clinton had "offended every country music fan" as well as all the folks like herself who'd "made it on their own, with no one to take them to the White House." Tammy had grown up on her grand-parents' farm picking cotton, okra, and beans, and later went to school to become a beautician. Once in Nashville, she co-wrote most of her songs and became the first woman to sell a million records.

She demanded and received an apology from Hillary, and,

like the lady she was, agreed to perform at a Clinton fund-raiser. After her death, the Clintons sent flowers and the president said, "Her trademark style has filled our hearts and made her a legend." It also made her funeral seem like a Nashville version of Princess Diana's. Fifteen hundred people crammed inside the Ryman Auditorium for the public memorial service, which was televised worldwide on CNN. She had sung about real people and real pain, to which she was no stranger. She said her stint on the short-lived soap opera *Capitol* was a natural: "My whole life's been a soap opera."

In addition to the multiple marriages, she had more than thirty major surgeries. She survived an infection in her intestines that put her in a coma, and did a stint at the Betty Ford Clinic for an addiction to painkillers, which was interrupted by emergency surgery at the Mayo Clinic. She was beaten and abducted from a Nashville shopping mall (and then accused of staging the whole thing for publicity), her daughter Georgette was the target of death threats, her daughter Tina was raped in Mexico, her tour bus (the Tammy I) burned to the ground, and she was forced into bankruptcy when a crooked savings and loan cheated her. It's no wonder that one of her favorite gospel songs was "Death Ain't No Big Deal," which gospel star Jake Hess sang at her private church funeral. "Life," says her friend and publicist Susan Nadler, "tore her up."

She was certainly fragile—and tiny, at five feet, four inches and a size two. Joanne Gardner, who was a masseuse before she became one of Nashville's top video producers, told me Tammy was covered with so many scars that "it looked like

Zorro had been after her." I once watched her put on one of the beaded dresses she wore onstage for a *Vogue* photo shoot, and she fell down beneath the weight of it.

But she was also a trouper. She was in the studio when told of Tina's rape, and she finished the track she'd been laying down. When her mother died in 1991, it was in the middle of a fan club cookout at her house, First Lady Acres. The fans were lining up for hot dogs outside, Leeza Gibbons was setting up to interview Tammy for *Entertainment Tonight* inside, and Meemaw, who had been unconscious for weeks, was hooked up to a respirator in a spare room off the kitchen. At the moment Tammy "introduced" Leeza to her mother, Meemaw took her last breath and Tammy fell apart, her mascara melting down her face. Gibbons offered to greet the fans in Tammy's place, but Tammy wouldn't hear of it. She pulled herself together and went out to hug, kiss, pose for pictures, and sign autographs. Finally, at midnight, she got on the bus and drove straight through to Canada for a single show, returning in time for Meemaw's funeral.

"You tell Tammy two hundred people want to see her in Branson, Missouri, and boom, she's on the bus," Susan Nadler told me at the time. Tammy always said she loved the road because it was "an escape from the real world." But it was more than that. She was of the generation of country entertainers who never stopped touring until the end, always thinking that but for the grace of God she might still be picking cotton.

She kept some cotton in a crystal bowl on her living room coffee table as a reminder, and her beautician's license, just in case. In her autobiography (titled, naturally, *Stand by Your Man*), there is a photograph of her enormous gold-fixtured bathroom at First Lady Acres, complete with a marble sunken tub, next to her first bathroom, an outhouse. Tammy's life was a lesson in grace and humility and guts. She stood by some of her men, and now one of them, Jones, is finally standing by her.

George Jones, Inc.

The first time I interviewed Tammy Wynette, I was greeted at the kitchen door by her fifth husband, George Richey, who was in the process of making sausage with biscuits and gravy, a classic combination. Richey's biscuits were homemade and his gravy was "cream," the kind made with milk and flour and sausage grease. Cream gravy looks a little too much like cat throw-up to me, but the sausage was good and so were the biscuits, and I was impressed that Richey, who is also a talented producer and songwriter, was doing his own cooking. (He was, too—when he checked the biscuits through the oven window, he grinned and said, "Oh yeah, those are gonna be award-winners right there.")

There has long been a connection between sausage and country music. The Louvin Brothers recorded the theme song for the Tennessee Pride brand almost fifty years ago; these days a new version can be heard on *The Grand Ole Opry* every Saturday night. In 1969, Jimmy Dean, whose hits include "Bumming Around" and "Big Bad John," started selling his own sausage, which quickly became the nation's number one brand.

Now, Wynette's third husband, George Jones, has introduced George Jones Country Sausage. Jones may well be the greatest country music singer who ever lived, and I am happy to report that his sausage is also excellent—well seasoned, with a good texture and just the right amount of fat. I went with him to an appearance at a Kroger supermarket near his house in Franklin, Tennessee, and the shoppers there, lured by the powerful smell of sausage frying in an electric skillet—not to mention the promise of an autograph and photo with Jones—packed the aisles. A female security guard told him she loved him, he bellowed, "Hello, Hazel!" into someone's cell phone, and an eight-year-old kid wanted to know what he'd been up to lately. "Not much," Jones said. "I get on the bus, I get off the bus. I go do a show, I get on the bus."

Apparently he's also been tinkering with his sausage. "They tried to cut the fat on him," Jones's wife, Nancy, tells me, referring to the Williams Sausage Company, which actually produces the stuff, "but George went on this rampage—he said it was too crumbly, it was too dry. He doesn't want to disappoint his fans." The finished product is available in three varieties—sausage and biscuits, patties, and "chub" (bulk sausage packed into a tube)—and two flavors, mild and hot. At the Kroger, Verbalene, the Joneses' housekeeper, piled an entire cart full of the sausage and biscuits, but I'm pretty sure they were mild—George says he'd "never heard of it hot until just a few years ago."

Jones has been in the dog food business and he has a line of steak sauces and marinades, but he is best known for his bad behavior, and, of course, for his voice. His hits include "He Stopped Loving Her Today" and "We're Not the Jet Set," a duet with Wynette in which he declares that "our steak and martinis are draft beer and weenies."

He will be the first to tell you that he "can sing anything." When I visited him at his house, a deeply awed Harry Connick, Jr., had just finished recording a duet with him for Connick's Christmas album (Jones had to be told who Connick was), and Jones burst out, unprompted, with an a cappella version of Don Gibson's "I Can't Stop Loving You" that brought tears to my eyes. That's the thing about Jones. He has a way of lingering on words and wrenching things out of them so that even if you did not speak the language you would know exactly what he was singing about. Frank Sinatra called him "the second best male singer in America," and Waylon Jennings wrote that "if we could all sing like we wanted to, we'd all sound like George Jones."

Jennings also told the journalist Nicholas Dawidoff, "Everybody says George Jones, he's an alcoholic. George Jones likes to get drunk. With all of us, it's 'Who's gonna tell me what to do?'" During most of the seventies and early eighties, the answer was no one. After his breakup with Wynette in 1976, his benders got so bad he says he had to be propped up onstage "like a mummy"—and that's when he turned up at all. He earned his nickname No Show by missing more than fifty concert dates in 1979 alone, and gamblers made book on whether or not he would materialize. He was arrested— a lot—for drunk driving and possession of firearms, he declared bankruptcy (in his autobiography, *I Lived to Tell It All*, he says he spent most of his money on cocaine, "foolishness," and cars) and finally ended up in a padded cell in Alabama. Nancy, who has been married to Jones for twenty years, is credited with cleaning him up. She sports a headlight-sized diamond ring, matching studs, and a diamond-encrusted watch, for which she makes no apologies: "I earned 'em."

Jones has indeed stayed mostly straight, but during a relapse a few years ago, he almost drove off a bridge a couple of miles from his house, and the police discovered a bottle of vodka in the car. A businessman bought the wreckage (but not the license plate, "No-Show 1"—Nancy's says "No-Show 2") and hung it, as a lesson to drunk drivers, from a construction crane in the middle of downtown Nashville. Jones himself is less sanctimonious. I ran over a driveway light on Possum Trail, the road leading up to his white-columned brick mansion, and when I confessed, he laughed and said, "Don't worry, hon, I'm partial to guardrails myself."

Each box of George Jones sausage features an apocryphal tale about the role that sausage has played in Jones's life and career, but the truth is he was never a huge fan of the stuff until he started hawking his own. Now, not surprisingly, he "dearly loves it." He grew up in the Big Thicket, an area in East Texas north of Beaumont where his daddy, George Washington Jones, was, variously, a moonshiner, a shipyard pipe fitter, an ice hauler, and, always, a drunk. The family, like most people in those days, made their own sausage out of whatever was left of the hog after the hams and bacon were smoked and cured. Jones says he "liked the smell of it when Mama would cook it," and that it was usually served with biscuits and "apostolic" gravy, a thin affair made by deglazing the pan with water. (Among other things, "Apostolics," the countrified name for members of the Pentecostal faith, are not allowed to chew gum, drink whiskey, dance, or drink coffee, which is what the far more flavorful redeye gravy is made with.)

Since his love of sausage came late in life, Jones professes to have no idea "what clogged these arteries up." He's had a quadruple bypass and his doctor called him on the morning of my visit with the news that his cholesterol was up. "WHOO! He liked to scare me half to death," Jones says. "And I don't eat hardly nothing." It is true that the only food visible in the Jones kitchen is a box of Ritz crackers and a bunch of bananas, but that's because he goes out for almost every meal. At lunch he heads to Subway or Jack-in-the-Box; at dinner, he prefers Stoney River in the Cool Springs Mall, where he generally orders the crab cakes, fried lobster tails, and steak. He is shocked when I tell him shellfish is high in cholesterol and protests that the lobster tails shouldn't be fattening since they're deep-fried, and, therefore, not in the hot oil for more than a minute or two. For a while a trainer came to the house, but he says he's been too busy with his sausage promotion to see him lately. "Besides that, he just about kills us. WHOO! I get so damn sore, I can't get out of bed for two days."

George says he allows himself a big breakfast with the sausage about once a week (the rest of the time he eats cereal). I tell him he ought to try my sausage balls, a suggestion that immediately becomes the source of great merriment. "Well, I've got the sausage and I've got the balls—HA! I couldn't resist." (He has finally warmed up to me because he has found out that I'm from Mississippi—when he thought I was from New York he refused to come home from the Subway.) "Yeah, we'll have to try to fix some of them balls," he says, before launching into an entire routine: "Say, Mama, they're burning up my sausage. Don't worry about your sausage, son. You better worry about your balls."

He is so tickled by the idea of the sausage balls that I tell him I'm going to name my version after him, and I have, though almost every cook in the South has a near identical recipe. It wouldn't do Jones much good, but they are delicious with cocktails.

George Jones Sausage Balls

YIELD: SIX DOZEN

1 POUND UNCOOKED GEORGE JONES HOT "COUNTRY-STYLE"
   SAUSAGE

10 OUNCES SHARP CHEDDAR CHEESE, GRATED

2 CUPS BISQUICK

Preheat oven to 400 degrees. In a mixing bowl, combine the three ingredients, making sure to work the sausage and cheese into the Bisquick well. There should be no dry crumbs.

With your hands, form into balls about an inch in diameter and place on a baking sheet. Bake until golden brown, about 8 to 10 minutes. Remove and serve immediately.

Tender Mercies

A few years ago, I was in my car in New Orleans when my mother called to tell me that the matriarch of a family to whom I'm extremely close had died. This woman had been ailing for some time, so the news was no surprise—and neither were the next words out of my mother's mouth: "You better go get a tenderloin." I was way ahead of her. I'd already turned the car around and was halfway to the grocery store.

My mother is forever toting tenderloins to the families of the sick and the dead. They are perfect, she says, because they don't take long to cook, everybody loves them, and they make excellent sandwiches (preferably on homemade yeast rolls with horseradish sauce). After I made mine that afternoon, I delivered it to the dead woman's house and hugged everybody and helped myself to some whiskey. Somebody picked up the last book she'd been reading with the place marked where she'd stopped, and we all reminisced about how superior her brain had been. The next day everybody drove to Mississippi, where she was buried, and where my mother had another tenderloin waiting.

The connection between tenderloin and tragedy is so ingrained in my psyche that the first thing I did on September 11, 2001, after I'd seen the first tower of the World Trade Center disappear before my eyes, was to go buy one. I was, obviously, in Manhattan, where I also live, and I'd been standing in the middle of Fifth Avenue in midtown. I hot-footed it back to the Upper East Side, bought the tenderloin from my friends at Leonard's Meat Market, went home, and called everybody I knew to come and eat it. I didn't need to call the Southerners in the group—within the hour they simply appeared in my living room.

Not everyone understands this connection between socializing and grief. In Eudora Welty's *The Optimist's Daughter,* the plot centers around the death of Judge McKelva and his daughter Laurel's reaction to it. Laurel was raised in the big old house in the fictional town of Mount Salus, Mississippi, where her younger, white-trash stepmother, Fay, now lives. Fay grew up in a trailer in Madrid, Texas, and she is horrified at the throngs of mourners already gathered when they return with the judge's body from the hospital in New Orleans. When she wails, "What are all these people doing in my house?" a neighbor ignores the question and explains instead, "You've got pies three deep in the pantry, an icebox ready to pop . . . and a dining room table that might keep you from going to bed hungry." Fay remains indignant: "I didn't know I was giving a reception . . . and who's making themselves at home in my parlor?"

Welty, as always, gets the details exactly right. Among the mourners are the members of the garden club, who, someone explains, "are a hard bunch to put off. They picked their flowers and they brought 'em." There are also the widowed Laurel's old bridesmaids, who meet her at the train station and set out the buffet, and the judge's friends, who make toddies and tell increasingly heroic tales about her father that Laurel is pretty sure never happened. The next day, burial day, the doings at the house are slightly more formal; the food is fancier. A chicken mousse is on the table, along with a Virginia ham supplied by the preacher's wife, who can't stop bragging about it. There's a coffee urn and a "silver tray heavy with some bottles and a pitcher and a circle of silver cups and tall glasses," and Fay's fat brother chomping on a seemingly perpetual ham sandwich. And there's Fay herself, of course, "resentment born," who takes off for Texas while the house is still full.

I felt a bit sorry for the awful, tight-faced Fay. There is no way she could possibly have understood the genteel, small-town subculture of flower-toting, casserole-making folks she was dropped into. I grew up not far from where Mount Salus is supposed to be, and I didn't fully appreciate it myself until I was seventeen and my paternal grandparents were killed in an automobile accident. They'd been driving back from seeing the dentist in Memphis when a truck hit them on Highway 61; I was home from school because it was Good Friday. My father's oldest friend came to tell us the news and my mother, just before she ran out the door with the two men, managed to yell, "Clean out the refrigerator and go get Tee." Tee was our maid and by the time I picked her up and got back, there were at least fifty people in our house: old men in their eighties, contemporaries of my grandfather's, stonefaced, sitting side by side on the sofa, brown bags of whiskey between their legs; my mother's friends clearing off the kitchen table and counters in preparation for the onslaught to come; women from our church taking turns at the back door with a notebook, so that later we would be able to thank the right person for the right pies and cakes and platters full of stuff.

Over the course of the weekend, I realized that there was a whole new category of food, funeral food. There were hams and roasts and, of course, tenderloins—not to mention dozens of casseroles topped with crushed Ritz crackers or crushed potato chips or canned Durkee's fried onions. I'd never seen a layered salad before, but there were at least a half dozen of them, featuring iceberg lettuce, frozen green peas, shredded Cheddar cheese, and mayonnaise (or Miracle Whip), each ingredient layered an inch deep in big glass bowls. There were frozen fruit salads, exotic concoctions made of canned fruit in syrup mixed with either Cool Whip or mayonnaise or both, along with marshmallows or nuts. I'd never tasted anything like them either, but not long ago, a friend gave me a copy of Mrs. S. R. Dull's *Southern Cooking*, first published in 1941. Mrs. Dull may well have been the source for much of the food that came through our door that weekend—there's a section on frozen salads that contains fifteen different recipes, including one for Frozen Fruit Salad No. 4, a mix of pineapple, cherries, grapes, mayonnaise, cream, marshmallows, and almonds.

It was much easier to concentrate on the food than what was actually happening. My father was devastated. His brother was dying of cancer and everybody in our extended family knew that they would be right back in the same spot, eating from the same covered dishes, in a matter of months or maybe weeks. There was not, after all, a lot we could say to each other. So we talked to everybody else. And if the conversation got too emotional or too long or simply too boring, there was always the endless supply of food around the dining room table. What a relief it was to go and graze on all those weird, cold salads, or to make a sandwich of the familiar tenderloin and take it outside on one of the dessert plates stacked up on the sideboard.

I have always joked that if I die, I hope it's in Greenville, because all my mourners would eat better. Lately, this has ceased to be a joke. When my aunt died recently in Nashville, we only got one layered salad and two platters of fried chicken, and the chicken came from the store. A sad day has come when the family of the deceased is reduced to take-out Chinese, the only thing on offer when I pulled into town that first night. Maybe it's an urban thing, because when the husband of a close friend died last year in New Orleans, my father was appalled at the number of deli sandwich platters, food that arrived on plastic trays and that, as he put it, "still had the price tag on it." My friend's husband was a precise cook and a man with a strong sense of how things should be done. I loved him and I couldn't bear the catch-as-catch-can quality of what was being set out on his table, so I decided to cook the entire lunch after his funeral myself. I had to, for his sake and mine, so I dragged my restless father to the grocery store, where I piled ten tenderloins and as many pounds of lump crabmeat into the cart. In the end, it all went so fast we had to pull out two auxiliary hams.

What was mostly missing that weekend were offerings lovingly prepared at home and brought over in Pyrex dishes or on silver trays, with the names of their owners written in capital letters on masking tape stuck to the bottoms. In the twenty-five years since my grandparents' funeral, I've been through so many deaths in so many towns that I can now match the name on the container with its contents without even looking. My friend Helen Bransford always makes a tray of tomato sandwiches with homemade mayonnaise because that's what soothes her in times of stress. Jessica Brent never fails to make her mother's amazing rum cake (she brought one to Helen, in Nashville, the night her brother died, the sole mourner bearing solace on a cake plate at ten o'clock at night). When another aunt was buried in Greenville, I arrived home to find Betty Joseph in the kitchen bearing her own tenderloin and a tin of cheese straws, and Bossy McGee at the sink washing lettuce for a salad.

I'm always hopeful that at least one person will turn up with one of those frozen fruit salads, maybe one with Bing cherries and cream cheese that I remember so fondly. As for me, I'm sticking with the tenderloin—my mother gave me one of her old silver trays with our last name still taped to it, so even if there's not a church lady manning the back door, I know it won't get lost.

Tough Love

"The good thing about Southern women," says my friend, the writer and cultural historian Henry Allen, "is that you have to match up to a standard of manliness. Southern women hold you up to this thing, which, you know, is your basic male standard. Which is, you gotta be willing to die for things."

Well, not so much anymore, but I know what he means. We come by this standard naturally. My father's close friend and business partner, J. B. Joseph, once wrote a memo to his daughters designed to help them assess "the strength of a man's commitment to certain values." (Or, as he put it to me later, to help them find a "sho-nuff man.") Among the questions he suggested they ask a prospective mate was "Have you ever in the line of duty (civil or military) voluntarily gone into a life-threatening situation?" And: "Have you ever in the line of duty (civil or military) ordered others into a life-threatening situation?" There were six more, about firing people and providing payrolls and taking tough positions and tithing to the church—all designed to show, if not what a man would die for, at least what he cared a whole lot about. After all, J.B. said, when "risking and sharing blood and treasure, there is no room for the abstract and the speculative." At the end, there was a warning: "Remember, there have been only two perfect men in history. One died on the cross for us 2,000 years ago, and the other surrendered at Appomattox Court House in April 1865."

No wonder we're demanding. This is pretty heavy stuff, especially if you just want to have some fun, but you have to admire the paternal impulse behind such a memo, and even some of its criteria ("Have you voluntarily served in political, civic, religious, or charitable organizations with no pay or little pay? Have you ever taken a philosophical position that was unpopular with your peers?"). I don't know anybody at this point who's holding out for Robert E. Lee—or even a tither—in these turbulent times, but it is true that Southern women are crazy about "sho-nuff men," and we are not big on the abstract.

In other words, we like a man who'll step up to the plate. Because we will. One Christmas after he wrote the memo, J.B. gave me a wildly popular T-shirt that read: GRITS: GIRLS RAISED IN THE SOUTH. I am too embarrassed to wear it (although apparently every woman at every beach resort below the Mason-Dixon line is not), but it is true. We have grit. We always have. The women of New Orleans were so rude to the troops of Benjamin "Beast" Butler (they spat on them and dumped the contents of their chamber pots on their heads) that he issued his famous General Order 28, the Woman Order, declaring that any female who treated his soldiers with disrespect would be "treated as a woman of the town plying her avocation." The Confederate men, knowing, in that case, exactly what they'd be willing to kill for, put a price on Butler's head.

Years ago, the novelist Padgett Powell wrote a wonderful piece in *Esquire* on the "allure" of Southern women. He told the story of a friend of his who married the woman he married because she showed a serious amount of resourcefulness and not just a little grit. They were bream fishing with catalpa worms and were doing so well they ran out of bait. The guy was desperate; the girl started tearing the worms in half. "On the first date," writes Powell, "he was sure any woman who would wordlessly volunteer to stretch bait in the middle of a bream frenzy was the girl for him."

Powell's friend was smart enough to recognize what was going on. Not every man is. *Webster's* says the antonym of grit is faintheartedness. A fainthearted person would not have been able to bring herself to pull worms apart. Likewise, a person who does have heart expects the same out of those she loves. If a girl is willing, and not even bothered by tearing bait in half, or shooing Yankees off the plantation, or whatever, the guy has got to at least look her in the eye, know what he's got there, and meet her halfway. Of course, a lot of times, a Southern woman is so capable, and so used to having to do things for herself anyway that she fails to notice that the guy hasn't met her challenge. This is the reason that most of my friends who got married are now divorced. They were too busy biting worms in half to notice that the guys were napping in the bow of the boat. One of the bravest and most compassionate women I know married one of the weakest men I have ever encountered. On one of the few occasions she displayed any weakness of her own, she got seriously sick in a restaurant. She had to ask her then husband to help her downstairs, which at least he did. She also had to ask him to go back up to get her some water, and he did that too. Except that when he got up to the table he found that their salads had arrived, so he sat down and ate his. By the time he moseyed back down, she had fainted in the parking lot and had gravel in her forehead. Needless to say, that was the end of that. My mother had already predicted the relationship's demise, rather too loudly, in the middle of the wedding ceremony. She's always right about that stuff. Plus, she knew he was from New Jersey.

Had he been raised by a Southern woman, or if he had had at least one other Southern girlfriend, he might have been able to rise to the occasion. On this point, I refer back to my friend Henry, who is also from New Jersey but who married a girl from Texas, which is close enough. Henry's theory is that a man becomes the strong, good guy that a strong, good Southern girl wants him to become. It has to do with our much-vaunted charm. "Charm is just fabulous and of course it works too," Henry says. "If she laughs at your jokes, then you think, 'Gee, I'm funny,' and pretty soon you are funny. You become what she guides you into being. This is what Southern women do. They pick up these wrecks—these besotted, alcohol-besodden, wounded wrecks. They pick 'em up and fix 'em up and send them out again." I asked him why he thought we bothered. "Southern women understand male pride. Unlike Yankee women, they want you to have some."

I asked J.B., the memo writer, who lives in Mississippi and is originally from Tennessee, if he had ever gone out with any Yankee women. "Not for long." Why not? "They didn't appreciate humor, or at least not mine." Humor is important, but it's not the point here. There should be a question on a memo regarding prospective female mates: "Would you be willing, for the sake of a man's pride, to pretend like you think his jokes are funny, at least some of the time?"

One thing about us, we will give you every opportunity. Things are pretty much yours to screw up. We are generous that way. We are generous in a lot of ways. Another story Padgett Powell told in his article was about the time he was having a drink at a hotel in South Carolina with two sisters, one of whom was his date. He asked his date if she'd like to go off and do some kissing. The other sister had been more or less deserted by the man she was with, so, to avoid being rude, he said, "Do you think your sister would like to go too?" His date didn't blink: "Ask her." So he did, and she said she certainly would.

The closest I have ever come to that particular kind of generosity is when I was seventeen and I got my boyfriend to kiss my best friend. He was so good at it, I wanted her to know what it was like. I figured they'd both enjoy it. That is the kind of behavior that gets you labeled stupid (what fool would loan out her very adept boyfriend?) or, worse, fast. It's not either, really. Both scenarios (Powell's and mine) have much more to do with appetite, with a certain straightforward gameness, with heart. "The unspoken question," says Henry, who has clearly thought a lot about all this, "is always, 'Are you up to it?' This is exciting." Yes, it is.

Queen for a Day

As late as the mid-1970s, a noted surgeon in my Mississippi hometown served as emcee at the Delta Debutante Ball, held every year on the first Saturday after Christmas. Before he officially introduced to society the dozen or so young ladies assembled at the Greenville Golf and Country Club, he gave a short speech. He explained to the debutantes that they were a part of a long and exalted and terribly necessary tradition—that of belles from the right families "coming out." He said society still had an especially useful function in the order of things (the implication being that the order of things had been in total chaos since the Civil War), and that by means of their very presentation that evening, the girls achieved "social attainment in the eyes of the Lord."

Few people—or at least few of the young ladies themselves—take debutante presentations quite so seriously these days, but debutante balls still thrive, especially in the South, where they are burdened with a whole lot of history.

The debutante as we know her is about four hundred years old, a creation of Elizabeth I, who began the custom of presenting eligible young women at court, and of Queen Victoria, who, almost three centuries later, included the daughters of the rising haute bourgeoisie along with those of the nobility and the gentry. Elizabeth II ended the practice after the last presentation in March 1958, but by that time the custom had made it across the Atlantic, where it was firmly entrenched. (Few people could tell you the name of an English deb from the 1950s, but everybody remembers Brenda Frazier.)

The first public presentation of debutantes in New York took place in 1870 at Delmonico's. Until then, debs had been feted at home (and, in New Orleans, young Creole ladies received at their family's box at the French Opera House), but Gilded Age magnates wanted to show off their wealth in public settings. In the impoverished postwar South, the presentations stemmed from different, more complicated motives—they were about emphasizing who had been well born before all had been lost. Such was the desperation to somehow resurrect high old times that the Montgomery, Alabama, Debutante Club was started in 1931, in the depths of the Depression. In the late 1960s and 1970s, when institutions like debutante balls briefly lost their cachet, the South's venerable clubs, like Charleston, South Carolina's St. Cecilia Society, remained as popular as ever. The balls were the means by which old families—and throngs of New South achievers—could tap into Dixie nostalgia and the myth of our cavalier past in all its full-blown weirdness. Presentations in New Orleans are more complicated still. In the nation's oldest city, the debutante is not just charged with recalling a lost culture (those good old days when women were safely on pedestals and lineage mattered most of all), she is also part of a still-thriving one: the secretive, Byzantine, often fantastic culture of Mardi Gras. Debutantes and Carnival are inextricably intertwined. The girls are not presented at court—they *are* the court of the mystic societies or krewes of Carnival, and they reign from Twelfth Night through Mardi Gras, complete with crowns and scepters. It all started in 1874 when the King of Rex (one of the original Mardi Gras krewes, or private men's clubs, which formed for the purpose of masking and parading) took his first debutante queen. The other krewes followed suit, and by the end of the century queens and their maids—and the elaborate and extremely hush-hush process of choosing them—had become an integral part of Carnival. Today, virtually all the girls who reign in the courts of the all-male, nineteenth- and early twentieth-century carnival krewes are still from "the coterie," says Henri Schindler, a Mardi Gras historian whose books include *Mardi Gras: New Orleans*. "The courts are debutante courts." While Carnival balls are not themselves debuts—there are two formal debutante societies, the Debutante Club and Les Debuts des Jeunes Filles de la Nouvelle Orléans, that take care of that—the balls launch mere debs to new heights. The courts of each krewe are covered extensively in the social pages of *The*

Times-Picayune, and the Queen of Carnival, who reigns over Rex, is always featured on the front page on Mardi Gras Day. Obituary writers, even now, find it necessary to remind us that the deceased was, say, Queen of Momus in 1942.

In Perry Young's *Carnival and Mardi Gras in New Orleans*, published in 1939, there is a chapter called "A Paradise for Debutantes." In it, he writes: "New Orleans Carnival is Elysium for debutantes and deliverance of their progenitors. Parties happen as everywhere and tremendous, but the fact is, and the consolation, that Carnival does everything that needs doing for every debutante, and with such delicacy, such splendour, such acclamation as no other mediary could approach, and spares the parentage those staggering difficulties, those ponderous disbursements they'd have to face to put over the young lady in any other climate—and for Mama such a fascinating game—making queens—as many as one little girl can be."

More than sixty years later, there is still plenty of splendor (if not actual Elysium) involved in being both a deb and a queen, but most of the young women will tell you that it also requires an extraordinary amount of stamina (and most of their fathers will take issue with Young's line about spared disbursements). "It's like an ordeal," says Blayne LaBorde, a twenty-year-old architecture major at the University of Virginia. "It's a lot of fun but it's definitely tiring." The season, which begins in August with Les Debuts, continues almost full throttle through Mardi Gras. The six months in between are packed with teas, luncheons, cocktail parties, dinner dances, more presentations, and private balls. At Les Debuts, the fathers, who are required to wear white linen suits, present their daughters, who are in traditional white gowns. "It's a simple process," says James Baldwin, president of the society. "Twenty to twenty-five young women are walked down the aisle on the arm of their father. They bow to their mother, curtsy to the crowd, and dance their first dance with Daddy. Then there's a breakfast and that's it. It's a private thing, a nice convivial way to get together." How did Mr. Baldwin, who is in the steamship business, get involved with Les Debuts? "Daddy," he answers, before asking and answering my next question. "How did he get into it? Daddy. I'm just fifth-generation Baldwin, that's all. That's how these things happen." Baldwin says that today "thirty or forty groups have a court," but everybody who is anybody can identify the old-line krewes. "It's diluted in a way. It's not the same as in the 1850s, when there would've been four or five balls and one girl would be queen of maybe two of them. Nowadays, if someone can't get into a club, they just form another club and little Lucy gets to be queen."

Blayne LaBorde got to be queen of the early-twentieth-century krewe Osiris because she was bright and beautiful, of course, but also because her father, Jack, has been a member for years, as had his father before him. LaBorde told me her reign was "more fun than I thought it would be. I honestly felt like a queen." It's no wonder. Her dress was so encrusted with pearls and rhinestones it weighed eighty pounds, and required a specially made metal corset to hold it up, along with her jeweled mantle and her ermine-trimmed cape. (Her mother, Peggy, tells me that each queen's dress typically requires more than forty hours of beading.) On ball day, her rigorous schedule included rehearsal with her king and court as well as hair and makeup. At about 5 P.M., dressed in her queen's regalia and holding her scepter (from a special scepter-making place in Mobile, Alabama), she began receiving at home. The crowd (which presumably included the more than two hundred people who had already paid homage to Her Majesty by delivering presents ranging from jewelry to picture frames) was so big that all the furniture had to be removed from her parents' spacious house. After being toasted and collected by two masked krewe lieutenants, she arrived at the ball in a limousine flying Osiris flags and accompanied by police escorts who actually stopped traffic. Upon arrival, she was given two masked attendants—in case, Blayne explains, "your dress gets caught or anything because you aren't supposed to move" on the throne.

After the invited guests are assembled, Blayne and her king, a man her father's age, make a lap or two around the Municipal Auditorium, are presented to the invited audience along with the maids and princesses (high school girls who will one day be maids and queens), and then the masked and costumed krewe members stage their "tableau," which basically means that they sort of gyrate around the place in their costumes. Next is the "call-out," during which the names of a handful of ladies are called out by the masked-and-costumed members of the dance committee, and these lucky women are actually allowed to get up and dance. Each one has a single dance with one of the costumed krewe members, who has just finished his own gyrating, and there are a total of eight dances. This ritual is not only elaborate but excruciating, since throughout the proceedings none of the women in attendance is allowed to have a drink (and even those male guests who are not krewe members must wait until a masker invites them to come have a nip behind the curtains). Finally, a whistle is blown, the dance committee clears the floor, the court takes another lap around the place, and then the whole, vastly relieved crowd repairs to the country club for the queen's supper, at which everyone is finally allowed to eat, drink, and dance with abandon, including the queen, whose torso was covered in bruises the next morning from the workout with her steel corset.

While Blayne's UVA roommate, visiting for the weekend, pronounced the whole spectacle "the coolest thing ever," Blayne herself told me later that "no normal human does this stuff." She is not entirely wrong. Mardi Gras balls are not normal events. The slightly bizarre nature of things does not stop with the balls, however. Because Blayne was a maid in Rex (the biggest, glitziest ball, which takes place on Mardi Gras night), she was only allowed to be a maid in the court of two other krewes, Mithras and Proteus, in addition to being queen of Osiris. Like Rex, each krewe has its own set of rules, each equally subtle and mysterious. "It's fabulous," says Schindler. "It's like China." Except that capitalism emerges triumphant. The average queen's dress costs from $6,000 to $12,000, says Judy Cobb, owner of New Orleans's Alice Designs, who made more than forty dresses for this past season, including Blayne's Osiris dress. Cobb's white "deb" dresses, worn at the presentation balls and by the maids in the Mardi

Gras courts, run from about $800 to $2,000, depending on the beading. (Blayne needed a total of six, so she bought four—including her "Cinderella dress," adorned with pearls and crystals—and wore two twice, after they had been significantly altered.)

Of course, the lineup of gowns doesn't begin to count the clothes she wore to the endless events in her honor—or any of her mother's gowns, including the red Vera Wang that Peggy wore to Proteus. ("Jack has been great," says Peggy. "He hasn't said a word.") Nor does it include the turquoise silk-wool suit and matching straw hat Blayne was required to wear in the viewing stand at the Rex parade. "Rex gives everybody a choice of a spring color," Peggy explains, and the girls must show up, like at Ascot, in a suit or dress with matching hat. "I know that sounds stupid but it's just part of the whole tradition."

I am learning about all this early on the Saturday morning before Mardi Gras. Blayne is sprawled on the couch, twelve of her UVA classmates have crashed upstairs, and Peggy is making cappuccino while I play with the ball gowns. The classmates will head north again on Monday, but Blayne has the Proteus parade and ball that day, and Rex on the next. But then she too will board a plane—at six-twenty A.M. Wednesday morning—for midterm exams. In case she's forgotten, Mom reminds her: "The debutante goes back to school on Ash Wednesday for midterms and we expect dean's list again."

I say something to the effect that anyone who can handle the activities, and the commute, of the last few months can probably handle that as well. Peggy agrees. "I don't want this to sound so fluffy," she says. "This used to be the high point of people's lives. Now it's just a fun thing to do. These girls are all very bright and focused individuals." Yes, they are. And for one short but grueling season, they uphold all that is sacred to their forefathers.

Miss Scarlett

The first time I saw *Gone with the Wind* was at the Belle Meade Theatre in Nashville, Tennessee. I was taken by my grandmother, and afterward, whenever I refused to go to bed or mind or otherwise acted willfully, she called me Scarlett. I was only eight years old, but I decided to take it as a compliment.

I adored Scarlett and her "passion for living" (Ashley's phrase), her refusal to give up, her absolute certainty that she would—somehow—get what she wanted. I was thrilled when she defied Mammy and convention and went off to the barbecue at Twelve Oaks "showing her bosom before three o'clock." I was impressed when she single-handedly saved Tara and then got rich running a sawmill better than any man could. (In the book, the men "swore silently" when she drove her carriage by.) As a child, I loved her because she refused to nap with the other young ladies and treated her sisters like the simpering irritants they were. I love her now for the same reason Rhett did, that she was "able to look things in the eyes and call them by their right names." And I have always been crazy about that chic green hat with the feather that Rhett brought her back from Paris when she was in "mourning" for poor, silly Charles, not to mention just about everything else she wore throughout the entire four-hour-plus movie.

Until that day at the Belle Meade, the only heroines I'd seen on screen were fairy-tale creatures like Snow White and Cinderella, pathetic figures, really, who kept waiting for their princes to come and save them. Scarlett didn't need a prince. She found that out the first time after Atlanta fell, and Rhett left her on the road to drive Prissy and Melanie and Melanie's brand-new baby all the way to Tara by herself. Ultimately, of course, she got one anyway. He wasn't always charming but he was gorgeous and funny and what every woman hopes for: a man who knows her, instinctively, inside and out, and loves her like hell just the same.

The Rhett/Ashley thing was the one part of her life Scarlett kept getting wrong, but by the end, she had finally learned her lesson. She'd also learned how to really love—another reason to admire her. It may have been too late, but I doubt it. James Michener once wrote an essay in which he compared Scarlett with Anna Karenina. Sure, they both—shamelessly—acted on their passions and flung them in the face of society. But Anna allowed herself to become a victim of her choices. Scarlett was never going to throw herself underneath any train. Early on she decided "she wasn't going to sit down and wait for any miracle to help her. She was going to rush into life and wrest from it what she could."

And then of course there are the unforgettable last lines of the novel: "With the spirit of her people who would not know defeat, even when it stared them in the face, she raised her chin. . . . I'll think of it all tomorrow, at Tara. I can stand it then. Tomorrow, I'll think of some way to get him back. After all, tomorrow is another day." She had known defeat, all right, but she would never be crushed by it.

When I first saw the film, almost thirty years had passed since its gala three-day premiere in Atlanta in 1939. But Scarlett was—and is—a quintessentially modern heroine. And the first accurate Southern one I'd ever seen. In her novel, which won a Pulitzer Prize, Margaret Mitchell used Scarlett and Rhett as positive, almost hopeful symbols of the postwar South. Yes, Scarlett loved the land, and almost killed herself to keep it, but she was not a woman who romanticized the false glory of the past (which, as she finally figured out, was Ashley's fatal flaw). All that "tomorrow" stuff was not procrastination or, heaven forbid, weakness. Scarlett was simply determined not to get mired down by defeatist ideals.

I'm pretty sure the term "steel magnolia" had not yet been coined when Mitchell created Scarlett, but she embodies the term better than any heroine since. She was a nineteenth-century feminist not the least bit shy about using her womanly wiles. Her petal-soft skin and gorgeous, "turbulent" green eyes belied an inner core that enabled her to shoot a Yankee without flinching. But when she needed the money to pay off Tara's taxes, she wouldn't have dreamed of asking for it wearing rags. The scene where Scarlett rips those curtains off the windows in order to fake a fine outfit is one of the most memorable images in screen history. She was Southern, she was a woman, she was going to keep up appearances. Only her rough hands gave her away.

But that rigged-up outfit symbolized more than just a desire to remain a lady of society; it was also about retaining some semblance of control. Scarlett's world had been turned upside down, but the outward display that everything was fine, even lovely, made it easier to feel that way inside. Margaret Mitchell understood the all-important effect of clothes and grooming; so did my grandmother, who possessed a whole lot of Scarlett herself. She would never have considered coming down the stairs in her own house without perfect hair and full makeup, without being dressed completely, with matching handbag and shoes and girdle and stockings and a serious amount of jewelry—even if she had no plans to leave the house. I never saw her actual fingernails underneath her Revlon Windsor enamel and she never failed to dab her pulse points with Bal á Versailles perfume, even when she took me fishing. And when she did go out on the town, she always dressed to the hilt in chiffon and furs and Delman evening shoes and little beaded peau de soie bags. She felt it was her responsibility to herself and those around her. That persona (people called her the Duchess) gave her strength when she didn't always want to muster any; it emboldened her to face the music or merely to face the day.

Likewise, Scarlett knew how to manipulate her beauty and create the necessary public image. She knew how to don a figurative suit of armor when she needed it and something more frivolous when she felt like it. Before running down the Twelve Oaks stairs to waylay Ashley, she was careful to stop and pinch her cheeks for color. After Charles died, she hated wearing the mourning clothes that tamped down her spirit. ("I just can't bear going around in black," she says, right after she sneaks a peek of herself in a purple-and-red-feathered hat.) Almost immediately after she gave birth to Bonnie, she was horrified by the thought of losing "the smallest waist in three counties," and had Mammy, against gravity and all odds, yank her right back into that cruel corset. Her pride in her clothes and her figure was part of who she was, part of her exuberance and lust for life. Rhett knew it from the outset— it's why his first-ever present to her was that green hat from Paris and the promise of a matching bolt of silk. Scarlett glowed in that scene. She could not wait to get herself wrapped up in all that finery.

Scarlett possessed in equal measure both grit and vanity. She would literally throw herself into the fields at Tara, but we also saw her clock plenty of quality time at her dressing table brushing her hair. In the end, that is the kind of woman I think most of us, at least secretly, want to be. We want to be resourceful enough to rustle up a stray pig for our starving kin's dinner. Or to create a useful gown out of our last useless vestiges of grandeur. That kind of woman, with all her strength and flexibility and passion and will, is not only interesting to men as wild and brave as Rhett, but to women as good and quietly strong as Melanie. That kind of woman also retains a remarkable hold on the public's imagination.

Indeed, more than sixty-five years after her debut, there are Scarlett Barbies and exorbitantly priced Scarlett collectible dolls. It is possible to buy—and wear—replicas of her "barbecue dress," her "red robe ensemble," and her "Peachtree ensemble." There is a Scarlett O'Hara cocktail (Southern Comfort, cranberry juice, and lime) and, naturally, a Scarlett O'Hara corset. There are websites devoted to her in almost every language, including Russian. According to one of them, there are even Scarlett impersonators in case "your future event might be enhanced by [her] presence." Rhett once told Scarlett that "with enough courage, you can do without a reputation." The same can also apply to style, and Scarlett had plenty of both. In these uncertain times, courage and style are two qualities well worth aspiring to. They are also timeless. After *Gone with the Wind*'s premiere, a reporter asked a nervous Margaret Mitchell if she had any thoughts. She said, "I'm so glad you liked my Scarlett." Of course we did. How could we not?

Member of the Club

Sometime in the early fall of 2001 (not long after 9/11), my friend Bobby Harling met me in Nashville, the city where I'd spent my childhood summers with my grandparents and where I still visit my various close friends and relations. Bobby had originally planned to stay for a night (there was a belated birthday party in my honor—I was born, alas, on September 11), but that was before we started eating. I think it was on the third day of his visit, and during our second meal at the Belle Meade Country Club, that he put down his fork and posed the question: "Why haven't I ever tasted this stuff before? Do they stop you at the city limits and check to make sure you're not smuggling out the food?"

Now, I had never thought of Nashville, or, more precisely, Belle Meade, as a culinary mecca. But in addition to being a screenwriter of note, Bobby is a prodigious gourmand, and he is not easily impressed. So when he brought it up, I realized that this privileged enclave (Belle Meade is actually an incorporated town within Nashville's city limits) had indeed made some unique contributions to American cuisine. These days, Belle Meade is best known as the place that produced our current Senate majority leader, Bill Frist, but the fact that it is also the home of the "frozen tomato," one of the world's great creations, should not be overlooked. The frozen tomato is essentially tomato ice cream (except, instead of cream, it's got cream cheese, cottage cheese, and mayonnaise), served in a round scoop on a lettuce leaf with a dollop of more mayonnaise on top, and Bobby was eating it when he started wondering why he had been deprived so long.

Nashville's culinary tradition has its roots in what can best be described as high WASP hotel (the kind of food that doesn't really exist anymore but that used to be found on ocean liners like the *Andrea Doria* and in hotel restaurants like Washington's late, lamented Jockey Club) spiked with a generous dose of (black) Southern soul. That is why at the same table on any given weekday in the Belle Meade Country Club, you will find ladies enjoying a cup of vichyssoise and nibbling on a date-nut-bread finger sandwich or a canned pear stuffed with cream cheese, but also scarfing down fried hot-water corncakes dripping with butter. During our visits to the club, Bobby and I ate platefuls of those same fabulous corncakes, along with the Faucon salad (iceberg and romaine lettuce topped with chopped hard-boiled egg, crumbled bacon, and "homemade bleu cheese dressing"), the Belle Meade Door

Knob (filet mignon atop a "toast crouton," accompanied by onion rings), and the Caramel Fudge Ball (an indescribably delicious scoop of vanilla ice cream rolled in extremely fine Oreo cookie crumbs and coated in butterscotch sauce). Then there were the possibly even more addictive corncakes (cooked on a griddle rather than fried) at Jimmy Kelly's restaurant and the glasses of iced tea we drank in my aunt's kitchen.

I realize that iced tea is not exactly novel in these parts, but in Nashville tea is not merely tea; it is a mysterious combination of tea, pineapple juice, orange juice, and mint, the individual formulas for which are known only to the cooks and housemen who contrived them. My grandmother's houseman, Lewis King, lived to be 102, and I must have thought—or hoped—he would live forever, because I never did ask him for his formula, which produced, naturally, the best fruit tea in all of Nashville. Lewis's daughter Ernestine made the finest corncakes, so light they were almost like crispy cornmeal quenelles, and so good that I would never sully her memory by trying to duplicate them. (Hot-water cornbread is one of those things, like biscuits and fried chicken, that are changed unmistakably by the hand of the cook who makes them.)

As a child who grew up in the very different social and geographical terrain of the Mississippi Delta, I thought Belle Meade was incredibly exotic. Our cornbread, for example, was a rather dry affair cooked in a black iron skillet, and our iced tea came only two ways—sweet or unsweet. Also, in addition to their own cuisine, the citizens of Belle Meade had their own language. To this day, carpools are referred to as "hookups," and garden hoses are called "hose pipes." I didn't even know there were real restaurants in Nashville until I was fifteen and got a driver's license. Until then, the only places I ever ate were my grandmother's table, the club, and Moon Drugs, where my grandmother and I went after she shopped for clothes at Grace's next door and where we always had chicken salad sandwiches and fresh orangeade. Sadly, Moon's is long gone, but the club's menu has barely changed—I recently saw a menu from 1950 that featured the Faucon salad.

There is no question that Belle Meade was—and in many ways, of course, still is—a closed society. (The June 1985 issue of *Golf* magazine included the Belle Meade club in an article titled "The 50 Snobbiest Clubs in America.") My grandmother was for years the secretary of the Gourmet Club, and after she died, my mother found the exhaustive minutes written in her elegant backhand. Much of them covered the half dozen or so meetings convened to discuss the controversial admittance of a single couple—a couple who had moved to Belle Meade from Minnesota. These Yankee interlopers, nice as they may have been, would not have known, after all, that iced tea is made with fruit juice, that a frozen tomato is not in fact a frozen tomato, that a Belle Meade Door Knob is not something that opens the door. In such a society, knowledge of that sort affords you a lot of leeway. Which explains why it was at the Belle Meade club that I first saw a man (who was not in a camp skit or at a costume ball) wearing a dress.

The man in question was Neil Cargile, Jr., and he was wearing a tennis dress, the old-fashioned kind, whose eyelet-trimmed bloomers peeked out from beneath the pleated skirt. Neil was later made famous (outside his immediate circle) by

John Berendt, who profiled him in a fashion issue of *The New Yorker* after I'd told him at a dinner party about Neil's late-in-life flirtation with cross-dressing. (He was in his fifties.) On this particular day, I had already been made to change my own clothes by my always-correct and perfectly dressed grandfather G. Daniel Brooks. After I'd put on something suitable, we went to the club and were on our way to a table when Neil, who was the son of an old friend of my grandfather's, passed by. Dan Brooks was not a man widely known for his open-mindedness, but when he saw Neil, he grinned and said, "Hiya doing?," slapped him on the back and kept going. I was speechless. Finally, I managed to point out that Neil, a burly, athletic sort, had on a dress. "I know that," my grandfather snapped. "He's been wearing them lately. Now come on."

I didn't dare bring up the subject again, but I could not wait to get to my aunt Frances's house to get to the bottom of things. When I got there, there was a Swan Ball committee meeting in progress, and the only thing my curiosity prompted was a question. "I wonder where Neil gets his shoes," one of the gathered women said. "I can't ever find any good-looking shoes in Nashville."

Neil died almost eight years ago, and I'm pretty sure the only people at the Belle Meade Country Club currently wearing dresses are the ladies, who since 1994 have been allowed in the Grill Room, but only after 6 P.M. Bill Frist resigned his membership in 1993 in preparation for his first Senate run, later explaining in a statement that as "a candidate for the U.S. Senate I simply didn't want to be a member of a private club since I am asking all Tennesseans to join my campaign." It was, obviously, a wise move, but I know he misses that frozen tomato as much as I do when I've been gone too long.

The Frozen Tomato

YIELD: 10 SERVINGS

3 CUPS TOMATO JUICE

3 CUPS HELLMAN'S MAYONNAISE

1 SMALL ONION, FINELY CHOPPED

¾ CUP CRUSHED PINEAPPLE

¼ CUP CREAM CHEESE

¼ CUP COTTAGE CHEESE

1 TABLESPOON WORCESTERSHIRE SAUCE

2 DROPS TABASCO, OR MORE TO TASTE

RED FOOD COLORING, IF DESIRED

SALT AND WHITE PEPPER, TO TASTE

BOSTON OR BIBB LETTUCE LEAVES

Combine 2 cups of the tomato juice, 1 cup of the mayonnaise, the onion, pineapple, cream cheese, cottage cheese, Worcestershire sauce, and Tabasco in a blender. Blend until smooth and pour into a bowl. Combine the remaining tomato juice and mayonnaise in a blender and blend until smooth. Add enough food coloring so that it is the color of a ripe tomato—otherwise it will be pale pink. Add it to the mixture in the bowl and whisk until combined. Season with salt and pepper and more Tabasco if needed. Pour into a 2-inch-deep baking dish (use a sieve if you want a smoother texture) and freeze.

Arrange lettuce on 10 salad plates and place 1 or 2 scoops of frozen tomato on top.

Add a dollop of mayonnaise if desired.

License to Kill

I happened to be in London in the fall of 1998 when Parliament voted 411 to 152 in favor of a bill to ban the "barbaric" sport of foxhunting with dogs. That first vote was what is called a "private bill," introduced by a single member, and essentially a poll to test support. However, since then, the practice has been completely banned in Scotland, and some sort of real "hunting with dogs" bill is being haggled over in England. It seems clear that foxhunting, at least in the manner in which it has been done for centuries, will not be with us much longer.

This is, of course, completely absurd. England without foxhunting would be like France without food. It is one of those necessary props, like the monarchy, that make the place different from, say, Indianapolis. Supporters of the ban maintain that the sport, in which people on horseback led by a pack of dogs chase but rarely get a fox, infringes on the moral dignity of man, not to mention the rights of foxes. This is a way of thinking that, as Bertrand Russell pointed out, "could logically end with the demand of votes for oysters." Since very few foxes are ever caught and killed in a hunt (six times as many are killed on the roads each year), one clever MP tailored her argument to address not just the rights of foxes, but their feelings. "I am not against killing foxes," she said. "What I am against is the chase. It is the cruelty involved in prolonging the terror of a living, sentient being which is running for its life." A slightly less emotional MP, a woman who had grown up on a farm, cited the fact that a fox had torn apart two guinea pigs belonging to a young girl in a London neighborhood just two nights earlier, and shared vivid childhood memories of the family chicken coop after a fox had dispensed with the chickens.

"Don't give me any romance about the pretty little innocent fox," she said. But romance is what we got. The MP who introduced the bill celebrated his victory by waving around a ludicrous stuffed-toy—and therefore very innocent—fox on the steps of the House of Commons.

This is not the kind of thing that would ever happen in Louisiana, where I'm currently sitting. I was amazed it was happening in England, but I couldn't get anybody I knew there appropriately outraged about it. They've gotten too used to this stuff, since the government has already banned bear baiting, badger baiting, and otter hunting, not to mention handguns. When a friend of mine from England visited me in Mississippi recently, it was the first time in her life she had ever seen a gun that was not in a policeman's holster.

Actually, there's not a lot of foxhunting in Louisiana. The closest we get is coon hunting, a rather different socioeconomic proposition in which guys in Lee jeans and orange jackets, as opposed to breeches and red coats, ride mules instead of horses. I have yet to hear a single person decrying the barbarism of a dog either treeing or tearing apart a "sentient, living" raccoon, an animal most people blame for tearing apart their garbage. But if somebody did and tried to make this form of recreation illegal, it would not go over big at all. Southerners historically have not reacted well to the government telling us what to do, especially if it is telling us to stop doing something as dear to our hearts as hunting. (In fact, our government tends to accommodate our desires in that area. When a local election in St. Mary's Parish once conflicted with the opening day of squirrel season, the election date was changed.) Also, we have a long tradition of simply killing the things that bother us.

Lately the people of Louisiana have been busy killing nutria. Nutria are disgusting-looking, orange-teethed, long-tailed rodents from Argentina who are partial to marsh grass. As I write, they are well on their way toward completely stripping about eighty thousand acres of wetlands between the Mississippi and Atchafalaya rivers, a problem Jefferson Parish sheriff Harry Lee decided to solve by regularly leading a pack of deputies on nutria-shooting expeditions and donating the carcasses to the lions at the Audubon Zoo. "It's very simple, very safe, very cost-effective. It's one shot in the head," Lee told reporters. "I fully understand some people think I'm a barbarian and I respect their opinion. But none of them have come up with a viable alternative."

In fact, there is an alternative, but I'm not sure how viable it is. The federal government has given the state of Louisiana $2.07 million to figure out how to market the nutria as people food. The theory is that if people want to eat nutria, they'll start shooting them like crazy. So far, the marketers have come up with changing the name to ragondin, the French word for "nutria" that, in my opinion, sounds a little too much like "rat." They have also pointed out how lean and healthy the meat is since the nutria feed only on grasses. Yeah, but nutria also swim in canals, and as one citizen said, "I'm not big on eating creatures that enjoy swimming in a mixture of water and petroleum products." Whether the nutria-marketing scheme works or not, I am proud to say that unlike the Brits, we do not enact laws to protect the feelings of our pests. We get government grants to figure out how to make more people want to kill them.

Also, unlike the Brits, we know how to keep our culture intact. During every Louisiana legislative session, someone introduces a bill to make cockfighting illegal, but since the state legislature is not Parliament, it always dies in committee. In one recent session testimony was given by two nuns about the detrimental effects on children who are allowed to attend cockfights, and a video was shown depicting what the New Orleans *Times-Picayune* described as the sport's "raw brutality." The committee chairman said he was unmoved by both the testimony and the video, which he did not think was "that bad," considering what chickens used for food production are forced to endure. The *Times-Picayune*, which did not sound nearly as alarmed by the gubernatorial candidacy of David Duke, who has advocated brutality toward blacks and Jews instead of chickens, demanded reform: "The roosters that die in cockfights die only to satisfy the blood-lusting, sadistic pleasures and gambling of the participants."

The participants at the one cockfight I've attended didn't seem to be filled with much bloodlust. They were regular folks passing time with the kids on a Friday night, drinking beer and making indecipherable two-dollar bets on some chickens with spurs on their feet. It was the night after Thanksgiving and everybody was enjoying, without any irony whatsoever, turkey-and-dressing plates for $3.95. The children seemed fine to me. Since most cockfights are interminable, they were given palettes to sleep on, and a sign on the door said NO CHILDREN ALLOWED OUTSIDE—it being infinitely more detrimental for a child to get hit by a car than to watch a cockfight, which in the end is not so much barbaric as boring. Apparently it takes a long time for a chicken who is not at the mercy of a fox to die.

It seems likely that chickens will continue dying in Louisiana cockfights because, despite the best efforts of the newspaper and the extremely small number of legislators who are animal rights activists, the state's cruelty-to-animals law does not include chickens. It did at one time, but, upon discovering that fact, the attorney general wrote an opinion saying that chickens are not in fact animals. They became "fowl" instead, which, in Louisiana at least, means that they can fight.

This is the kind of lawmaking I like. Somebody says we can't have cockfighting because there is already a cruelty-to-animals law on the books. The attorney general says, "Okay then, a chicken's not an animal anymore," and about ten years later the state legislature passes a law saying the same thing. The breathtaking simplicity of this method of operation is complicated slightly by the fact that, under the law, not all birds are fowl; some get to stay animals. This is really true. The law reads, "Fowl shall not be defined as animals. Only the following birds shall be identified as animals for purposes of this Section." And then it lists the lucky ten: "parrots, parakeets, lovebirds, macaws, cockatiels or cockatoos, canaries, starlings, sparrows, flycatches [sic], mynah or myna." In other words, if you're a bird and you can talk, you're in luck.

Now, I want to know how the representatives of the people of the state of Louisiana arrived at that list in committee. Did somebody say, "Okay, we can't have any lovebird torture around here. But hell, woodpeckers—I don't give a damn." How did they determine that it is okay to stick an ice pick through the skull of sweet little Robin Redbreast, for example, when starlings, birds my own mother shoots on sight, are protected as animals?

Apparently, some fowl torture has always been acceptable. It is even a theme of sorts in Southern literature. A character in Truman Capote's *Other Voices, Other Rooms* collects the wings of bluebirds his stepmother kills for him with a fire poker. Then there's *To Kill a Mockingbird*, in which Atticus tells Scout and Jem not to shoot mockingbirds but that blue jays are fair game.

With the exception of *Aesop's*, there is not a lot of fox literature from any region. In *In Another Country*, Hemingway wrote about some foxes but they were dead. They were hanging out in front of a butcher's stall in Milan. I think Hemingway just wanted to describe the wind blowing those foxes' tails and the "snow powdered" in their fur, because I have never heard of anybody actually eating a fox. Oscar Wilde said it couldn't be done. But maybe those mistreated English foxhunters ought to try it anyway. They could change the name to "renard" and market it to the masses as something good to eat. Then maybe nobody would care how the poor things died.

Bird Song

To the Southerner, there is simply no other food that possesses the stature of fried chicken. It cuts across class lines (when I was growing up, if we were dressed in church clothes, we'd eat it at the country club; if not, we'd mingle with the masses at KFC and take home a bucket from the Colonel). It cuts across regional lines (unlike, say, gumbo, which is enjoyed in other states, but does not retain the same exalted rank outside of Louisiana, or pilaf, which is relatively unheard of beyond South Carolina). It can also be the subject of intense debate. For example, should the chicken be marinated overnight in milk and seasonings before it is placed in a paper bag and tossed with flour, or simply washed and dried first? What should the seasonings be? Also, should the chicken be fried in lard or oil? Most cooks I know have passionate, unequivocal answers to those questions. And just about everybody I know has his or her own highly personal benchmark, the standard against which all other fried chicken must be measured.

For my friend Rick Smythe, it's the chicken at Fratesi's, a store on Highway 82 near Tribbett, Mississippi, where they've been frying chicken at least as long as Rick's been alive. There, the chicken is soaked in a mixture of milk and water, coated in flour seasoned with onion salt, garlic salt, Season-All, and black pepper, and fried in oil at 350 degrees Fahrenheit. Last time I was home Rick insisted I try it (like most people with a benchmark, he wants you to understand why it became one), so I sampled four pieces until there was nothing left but bones. When I told our mutual friend Ralph McGee that I thought Fratesi's chicken was indeed pretty tasty, Ralph looked at me like I was crazy. "It ain't nothing like Lola Belle's," he said, and so it goes.

Lola Belle was the McGee family cook. Lottie Martin was ours, and she really did cook the best fried chicken in the world. And even though I conservatively estimate that I ate more than a thousand pieces of it before she died, I cannot tell you what made it so good. Great fried chicken has an ineffable quality. The cook's hand probably has at least as much to do with it as, say, black pepper versus cayenne. But when everything somehow comes together just right, there is nothing better in this world. Still, it's hard to explain. The only person I know who has accurately articulated the feelings that good fried chicken inspires is my friend Jimmy Phillips. Like Ralph and Rick and me, he grew up in the Mississippi

Delta, and for a while he was a songwriter in Nashville, where he wrote "Fried Chicken" and recorded it as a single. He also recorded a really great album that boasted liner notes from no less a personage than Peter Guralnick, but Jimmy left Music City behind and currently hides his light under a bushel by running a ski lodge in Telluride, Colorado. None of us can understand this since Telluride is 10,000 feet above sea level and is not, to my knowledge, remotely famous for fried chicken. Fortunately, Ralph McGee still lives in the Delta, below sea level, where he farms and plays a mean guitar. Pretty much every time I go see him, he plays "Fried Chicken" for me, preferably after we've just eaten some.

Since I've always thought the song deserves a wider public, I'm offering the lyrics here—with Jimmy's permission, of course, along with a few explanatory notes of my own:

It was high noon, Arcola, Mississippi, another Sunday feast
Popped my head into the kitchen and I heard that gurgling
    grease
I said, Georgia, what you cooking?
She said, Jimmy, what you think?
You better come on in this kitchen and wash your hands up in
    the sink
'Cause we're having

Fried chicken
Wing takes a breast, leg takes a thigh
Rice and gravy, black-eyed peas, and corn bread on the side
It's a Southern institution

Black skillet is preferred.
Fried chicken: a most delightful bird

Well, first of all, the "gurgling grease" line is a genius stroke. People's hearts skip beats when they hear that sound. It is also useful. When the grease is at the right temperature, a little corner of a piece dipped into it will get that grease gurgling like crazy. That's how you know it's time to slide the rest in. Second, "black skillet" is definitely preferred, if not required. A heavy cast-iron skillet that has been cured over the years, developing that almost menacing blackness (Ralph named his black Labrador "Skillet"), will cook the chicken more evenly, and lend it a deeper color and flavor. Properly seasoned skillets are so valuable that they are handed down from generation to generation, but, fortunately, it is easy to season your own. It just takes time—and a lot of chicken.

When we sat down at the table, it was glorious to see
All that knuckle-sucking goodness just looking back at me
Grandmama said the blessing but I could not concentrate
For I had visions of drumsticks dancing in my plate
Thinking 'bout that

Fried chicken . . .

If you have not been enlightened
May I hasten to explain,
Full awareness is heightened
When the grease goes to your brain

Fighting over white meat, loser gets the wing
I declare I love that chicken more than anything
Pass the fresh tomatoes, man, I just can't stop
And don't forget the sweet potatoes with marshmallows on
    the top
To complement that

Fried chicken . . .

The side dishes in the chorus and the last verse are typical accompaniments, although there is very little that doesn't go well with fried chicken. I love it with potato salad and green beans cooked with ham hocks, and I'm strongly in Jimmy's camp where the sliced tomatoes are concerned. Lottie always served her fried chicken with mashed potatoes and yeast rolls, but some people are more partial to biscuits (hence the gigantic, greasy, and actually pretty good examples available at Popeye's and KFC). The other night I served it with corn pudding, but anything equally sweet and starchy—Jimmy's sweet potatoes, summer squash casserole—is a good counterpoint to the crispy saltiness of the chicken.

I would be remiss here if I didn't address some of the subjects that cause disputes among fried chicken cooks. In several recent taste tests I conducted on some willing participants, we all agreed that the chicken that had been soaked overnight in buttermilk was by far the tenderest. Some people don't dry the milk off and dip the chicken into the flour wet, which makes a crunchier batter that holds up better cold. I dry mine off. I also stick with the basic seasonings of plain old salt, black pepper, and red pepper (with a bit of paprika for color). For frying, I know old-timers and sticklers who won't use anything but lard. I'm sure it is superior, but vegetable oil and vegetable shortening are a heck of a lot easier to find. Melted vegetable shortening, which is what Lottie used, is more refined and leaves less odor.

All that said, I don't think I've ever had a piece of bad fried chicken. You just have to be brave that first time at the stove. Or, you can always go out. Among my personal favorites are Sherman's in Greenville, Mississippi, a former grocery store where I ate the great majority of my chicken after Lottie died and where it is still mighty delicious; the Four Way Grill in Memphis, Tennessee (on, naturally, Mississippi Street); and Jacques-Imo's in New Orleans. Last year I ordered 150 pieces from Jacques-Imo's for my good friend Anne McGee's surprise fortieth birthday party (she is Ralph McGee's first cousin and her favorite food is fried chicken—and yes, he came to the party and sang the song). The restaurant received a high compliment when many of the guests assumed the chicken had come from my own kitchen. It's not that I'm a particularly great fried chicken cook, it's just that home-cooked chicken nearly always trumps a restaurant's. Especially a restaurant where the chicken, of necessity, is cooked in a deep fat fryer. As Calvin Trillin has observed, "A fried chicken cook with a deep fryer is a sculptor working with mittens."

Which leads me to another of my top fried chicken places, Prince's Hot Chicken Shack in Nashville, Tennessee. My friend Joe Ledbetter turned me on to Prince's one night by forcing me to try each of their three flavors, regular, hot, and extra hot. The extra hot will kill a normal person—at least half a bottle of cayenne pepper coats each piece. But the regular (still plenty hot enough, believe me) is a truly superlative example of what fried chicken should be. After the first bite I said, "This was fried in a skillet." Joe assured me that it had been. Then we all got quiet and went to work eating. It was the closest to Lottie Martin I had felt in twenty-six years. That ineffable something had happened, that magical, unexplainable thing that makes fried chicken, as Jimmy Phillips always ad-libs when he sings the last chorus to his song, "a most delightful, quite exciteful bird."

Fried Chicken

1 FRYING CHICKEN, ABOUT 3 TO 3½ POUNDS, CUT INTO
   8 PIECES

BLACK PEPPER

2 TEASPOONS SALT

1 TEASPOON PAPRIKA

1 TEASPOON CAYENNE PEPPER

1½ CUPS ALL-PURPOSE FLOUR

LARD, VEGETABLE SHORTENING, OR VEGETABLE OIL

Put the chicken in a basin of cold water, soak for a few minutes to remove any traces of blood, and dry well. Season with salt and black pepper. Mix 2 teaspoons of salt, the paprika, and the cayenne into the flour. Put the flour in a brown paper or large Ziploc bag. Add a few chicken pieces at a time and toss well until coated. Remove and shake off excess flour. Over medium-high heat, melt enough vegetable shortening or lard to come to a depth of 1½ inches in a heavy skillet, preferably black iron. When the fat has reached about 350 degrees, slip the chicken pieces in, dark meat first, being careful not to crowd them. (Test the temperature with a candy thermometer, or dip a small corner of a chicken piece into the fat—if vigorous bubbling ensues, the temperature is right.) Turn the heat down to medium and cook for ten minutes.

Turn the pieces with tongs and cook until the second side is browned, about 10 to 12 minutes more. Drain on brown paper bags or on a rack placed over paper towels.

To Season a Skillet

Preheat the oven to 200 degrees. Wash a new cast-iron skillet (found at most hardware stores) well with a mild soap. (This will be the first and last time the skillet will be touched by soap of any kind.) Rinse it well and dry thoroughly. Rub the inside of the pan generously with lard, olive oil, or vegetable oil. Place in the preheated oven for one hour. Turn off the oven and leave the skillet inside overnight. The next morning, wipe the skillet out, and repeat the process. The skillet is now ready for cooking. After each use, wipe it out, rinse lightly if necessary, and wipe it dry. If food sticks to the pan, use a nonabrasive plastic scrubber or a pinch of salt to get rid of it, and rub the spot with a bit of olive oil.

A Plague on Our Houses

Recently, in *The New York Times Magazine*, I saw an ad for something called a "plagues bag." The copy billed it as a "Passover Seder enrichment toy for parents and children to enjoy together." There was a number, 1-888-PLAGUES, so I called it. The woman on the phone told me that for $10.95 I could get a burlap bag full of items illustrating what the Lord let loose on the poor people of Egypt so that the Pharoah might be moved to let His people go. The bag, she said, included a handful of Styrofoam hailstones, a vial of "red stuff" representing the rivers that turned into blood, a "hoppy frog," a locust, and a plastic egg filled with little-bitty plastic lice. She couldn't remember what else was in there (and I didn't ask her what had been selected for "boils upon man and beast," or if miniature replicas of the slaughtered firstborn were featured), but she did describe the whole package as "really, really adorable."

Sadly, the bags are back-ordered, so I'll have to take her word for it. I was curious about them because I live in New Orleans, where, like every other place in the Deep South, we have a lot of plagues, though none that I would describe as adorable. We have hurricanes and floods and all manner of pestilence, not to mention extreme heat, humidity, alligators, and snakes. When the colony of Louisiana was founded by Iberville in 1699, a priest in the first settlement marveled at mosquitoes so "prodigious" the men "could not distinguish one another at a distance of ten paces." The acting governor, Sauvole de la Villantray, wrote that "there is such a great supply of alligators that one sees them at every moment," but that "the snakes are much more dangerous." He reported that "June is the hottest," the land is "nothing but burning sand," it rains every day in July, and without the wind out of the southwest, "we would surely perish." He did perish, a year later, along with about a third of the other colonists, and things haven't improved much since. In fact, they've gotten worse.

A new plague is being visited on the people of New Orleans in the form of an infestation of Formosan termites. These are not normal termites—experts use words like "devious" and "aggressive" and "freaks of nature" to describe them. They eat wood nine times faster than the subterranean termites we are used to, and they grow far bigger colonies. A record-breaking colony of seventy million was found underneath a public library here, and even larger ones are suspected in the French Quarter. Unlike most insects living in colonies, they don't compete; they actually help one another, and they can live anywhere: beneath houses, at the tops of high-rises, in attics, in trees. They eat through anything: insulated electrical wires, creosote-coated utility poles, brick mortar, caskets. They ate the clock at the top of the 185-foot wooden bell tower at St. Patrick's Cathedral, so now there's a plastic one. No structure is immune—but they are. So far, nothing has been found that will kill them.

When I got here several years ago, I had never heard of a Formosan termite. New Orleanians themselves didn't find out about them until about thirty years after their arrival in the 1940s, courtesy of the same folks responsible for most of the other terrible things inflicted on the South—the federal government. Native to China, the termites have been around for about a hundred million years, and by the 1500s they had spread to Formosa and Japan, where citizens referred to them as "do-toos," destroyers of shrines and temples. After World War II, they hitched a ride to New Orleans in crates and scrap wood on ships returning home with military equipment. By the time anybody noticed them, the creatures had dug in, and the only possible chemical that might have kept them at bay had been banned. In the late 1980s, a Louisiana State University entomologist thought he'd finally figured out a way to get rid of them, but then he fell victim to another New Orleans plague—street crime. He was murdered for his wristwatch on his way home from celebrating an agreement with city officials that would have enabled him to test his treatment.

In the decade or so since, the termites have done more damage to New Orleans than hurricanes, tornadoes, and floods combined. The newspaper is constantly full of nightmarish stories: an infested live oak falls on an exterminator's truck and crushes it; a man's house splits in two—while he's inside it; a couple move into their dream home to find it "being eaten around us." It's heartbreaking stuff, but what really makes people lose their minds is the swarming season. To walk under any streetlamp during the months of May and June is to be attacked by hundreds of mating termites. When their wings fall off, they drop on top of you and crawl inside your clothes. They chase Little League teams off the field, ruin hundred-thousand-dollar outdoor wedding receptions, force entire neighborhoods to crouch inside their homes in the dark.

The first year they swarmed inside my house (they swarm from within and without), I had no idea what was going on so I tried everything. I turned off the computer, the TV, the lights. I walked around with a candle and a can of Raid, which didn't do a thing except make it impossible for me to breathe. I killed them one by one with wads of wet Kleenex until I realized there were far more of them than I had Kleenex. Finally, I decided to drink enough wine (two bottles) to keep me from caring that they were crawling on my pillow. The next morning an entire beam in the attic was gone.

It wasn't a complete loss. At least I cracked the riddle of why everybody down here drinks so much. In his journal, Sauvole complained that his men were always drunk, but had he joined them, he might have lasted a lot longer. Sauvole, bless his heart, was a poet from Paris. I imagine it was a tad difficult to make the transition from the boulevards and cafés to the burning, plague-ridden sand. Newcomers still have a tough time of it. A hundred and fifty years after a traveler named Josiah Gregg called New Orleans the "graveyard of the United States" and pronounced the air "unhealthy" to breathe, former New Orleans Saints coach Mike Ditka echoed his sentiments almost verbatim. Chief among Ditka's complaints were that the streets smelled bad and there was no place to buy a good suit, which enraged everybody because despite the fanfare of the expensive new coach's arrival, the Saints continued to lose. Also, he lived in a swank new sub-division across the river where the termites hadn't even made it yet.

I used to joke that living here is much like living in the Old Testament. But the ad for the plagues bag sent me back to the Bible, and I have revised my opinion. We have it much worse. Take the locusts God sent to Egypt. They were not nearly as bad as our termites. For one thing, they only ate vegetation and we have buck moth caterpillars that do that. John Benton, owner of Bayou Tree Service, swears the cater-pillars were so bad a few years ago that he could hear them chewing. They are covered with spines that are toxic and dangerous even after they are killed, so that when they fall off the trees, Benton says, "they are like little land mines on the sidewalks. If you look at them under a magnifying glass, they are like something out of a science fiction movie."

When the Lord decided to smite Egypt's borders with

frogs, He sent them into houses, bedchambers, ovens, and "kneading troughs." As unpleasant as that must have been, frogs—unlike alligators and snakes—generally do not kill people. Sauvole was hardly the only settler to mention the snakes, he was just the first. Pierre Clement, Baron de Laussat, the last colonial administrator of Louisiana, actually apologized for his lengthy "digression" about snakes in his 1803 memoirs, but he couldn't help it—they had made a big impression on him. He attended an outdoor dinner party for fifty and just as everybody was being seated, "a snake fell from the trees and was promptly killed." His cook went to the yard to pick up a "setting turkey" and "found his bare arm immediately entwined by a large puff adder that was eating its eggs." Sixty years later, the place was still teeming with them. A Yankee soldier complained during the siege of Port Hudson, "I don't suppose there is a spot on earth where there are so many snakes to the acre as right here."

The lice didn't bother the Yankees nearly as much: "We just boiled our clothes and that was the end of them." The mosquitoes were another story. "If I had a brigade of men as determined as these Brashear City mosquitoes," wrote the same soldier who had marveled at the snakes, "I believe I could sweep the rebellion off its feet in a month's time." A century later they hadn't gone anywhere, so in 1963 a twenty-four-member Mosquito Control Board (now renamed, not surprisingly, the Mosquito and Termite Control Board) was set up in New Orleans to see what it could do, which was not a whole lot. In one of his typically enlightened moments, Leander Perez, the notorious boss of Plaquemine Parish, advocated incarcerating civil rights protesters—outside—at Fort Jackson. Somebody reminded Perez that Fort Jackson had already been leased to a cattle rancher, but there were so many mosquitoes the cattle inhaled them and choked to death.

Also, the plagues in Egypt lasted only seven days. Ours never end. This summer, for example, June started off at 98 degrees, breaking an eighty-seven-year-old record. I know snow and ice is terrible too, but the good thing about cold weather is that it kills things we can't get rid of down here, or at least it slows them down a little. We haven't had a freeze in so long the snails have become bionic—they practically glide across the hundreds of dollars' worth of snail bait I have dumped in my garden. The slugs are so huge, one of my neighbors wakes up in the middle of the night to chop them up with a machete.

Given the state of things, it's no wonder the first settlers pined for the mother country. The Baron de Laussat wrote that they "spoke frequently of France." I guess they did. I wouldn't mind going there myself. But lately, I have been thinking more of Finland. A couple of summers ago, my friend Peter Patout and I were driving along in Harahan, Louisiana, a sort of suburb of New Orleans. It was a normal summer, with a rainfall of at least seven inches a month. The drainage in Harahan is not so good and the downpour we got caught in became a mini flash flood, which wouldn't have been a problem if the parking lot I thought I was turning into hadn't turned out to be a twelve-foot-deep canal. I had been thinking a lot that summer about Mary Jo Kopechne—no joke—because it was the twenty-fifth anniversary of her death, and it had been in all the papers. Every time I read about what happened to her, I decided if it ever happened to me, I would damn sure try to get my door open in time. And after a bit of trouble I did. We swam out and pulled ourselves up on the bank, and by the time we turned around all we could see was the car's trunk bobbing up and down. Peter is extremely good-natured, and since he was born in Louisiana, he was also smart enough to have packed his clothes in an ice chest. The car was a total write-off, but it wasn't worth much in the first place, so we laughed and posed for pictures taken by some stranded Finnish tourists, who were, ironically enough, on their way to a swamp tour where they hoped to view lots of alligators. Anyway, a few months later, at Christmas, they sent the pictures to us with a note suggesting we come to their country for a visit. There is, they said, little danger of flash-flooding in Finland.

That's Entertainment!

Several years ago, in Seaside, Florida, I put on a beach pageant starring my niece, who was then six, as a kidnapped mermaid, a slightly more reluctant but extremely sweet and patient friend as an evil catfish, and me as the good sea witch. The narrator was my friend Courtney, who sang new lyrics to the theme from *Gilligan's Island*. Courtney and I are both grown people but we had a grand time cruising the aisles of Wal-Mart for costume materials, and we bought so much at the shell shop that the cashier asked us if we were activities directors at a resort. When we finally performed, after days of glue-gunning and hours of rehearsing, it was for an audience consisting of my mother, my sister-in-law, and my other niece, who had just turned one.

Now, this seemed to me and everybody else involved

(with the exception of the evil catfish, who had to have a few drinks to prepare for his role—as well as for his costume, which featured blue pipe-cleaner whiskers and flippers worn with white socks) to be a perfectly normal, even desirable thing to do. The people in Seaside thought otherwise. Seaside is a made-up town on a gorgeous stretch of beach that has, until recently, been affectionately called the Redneck Riviera. Almost all the people who vacation in Seaside's extraordinarily expensive houses are from the South, but by virtue of the fact that they are there, they ain't rednecks anymore and they don't want to be mistaken for any. They drive really nice cars (Lexuses and luxury SUVs) and wear really nice clothes (a great many of which boast Seaside's embroidered logo) and a lot of them are too uptight to even make eye contact with their neighbors. Things have loosened up a bit since that first pageant (for one thing, we've put on about six more). But that summer, they did not understand what we were up to.

As soon as we walked outside, traffic stopped. Children screamed. When one brave kid on a bike said he was going to go see what we were up to—or, indeed, what we were— another kid started hollering for his daddy. Admittedly, we were a sight. I had made a very tall tiara out of palmetto leaves and starfish and had dried sea horses hanging from my ears. The evil catfish had been turned evil by the fishing hooks and (plastic) bait hanging all over his Brooks Brothers shirt. Courtney's headgear featured an openmouthed (dead) alligator anchored down by a tinfoil headband covered in red and purple glitter. And my niece, in her aqua eye shadow, shell-encrusted bustier, and silver lamé tail, looked alarming like a contender for Little Miss World.

Now, if I'd seen people looking like we did I'd have followed right along behind them, but the only followers we got were dogs. When we went for a post-pageant drink at the packed beachfront bar, those people who weren't so embarrassed that they ignored us altogether wanted to know if we'd been in a movie. We said no, we'd just put on our own little show, so they asked if it had been open to the public. And we said, well, you know, it could've been, but nobody seemed particularly interested, and that, really, we had just done it to do it. That is what they could not understand. "But why?" they kept asking. "What made you want to?"

Until that moment I had not realized how few people are familiar with the concept of entertaining themselves. The other day I was listening to a radio interview with a ninety-year-old Ms. Senior Virginia contestant whose talent was telling about first ladies and whose evening gown was a velvet hoop skirt. When the guy from National Public Radio finally got around to asking her what I knew he could not fathom— why on earth she would participate in such an event—I could just imagine the "I-feel-sorry-for-you-young-man" expression on that woman's face. "You have to do something to entertain yourself, you know," she said, adding that she also had three married boyfriends.

In the Mississippi Delta, where I'm from, entertaining yourself is a high art. There isn't anything else to do. You sit around in what was not all that long ago an uninhabited swamp looking at mud and sky all day, and you learn at a young age the trick that has kept that old lady from Virginia alive this long: Entertain yourself or drink yourself to death. Often, of course, the two are intertwined, a tradition dating back to the days when there was even more mud and a lot less people (the first white settlers didn't arrive in much quantity until around 1825). In his book *The Most Southern Place on Earth*, James Cobb excerpts the diary of a man who attended three all-night parties in the space of three days in the Delta of 1887. He endured stifling heat, long carriage rides, and at least one train trip in order to "gyrate" until well past dawn, an activity that shook the foundation of one house and produced "ceaseless yells" from the baby in another. Each "shindig" was respectively pronounced "uproarious," "tremendous," and "a glorious victory." Only his feet, too swollen from dancing to fit into his shoes, prevented him from attending a fourth.

All this relentless self-entertainment is worthwhile because if you do it really well, you can get a lifetime of future entertainment out of it. Because you've got a story. As in, "Hey, Courtney, remember that time you glue-gunned those big green scallop shells to your bra and sang that mermaid song?" After that, the whole afternoon is filled up.

People are always asking why there are so many writers from Mississippi. And the kind of people who are supposed to know always say it's (at least partly) because of our habit of storytelling. Well, yeah. *Absalom, Absalom!* is a long story about a story. One good thing about Faulkner was that not only did he write great stories but he also was a character in a few of his own. ("Remember that time he came to Greenville to play tennis with Will Percy and got too drunk to play and then he . . . ?")

My mother's friend Bossy had an impromptu party one Sunday afternoon at which a wedding "rehearsal" was staged for two of the guests who were about to get married. Everybody got all dressed up in whatever they could find in Bossy's closet, which in the case of our friend Simpson Hemphill was a caftan and a shower cap with lots of plastic flowers on it. Simpson had just begun playing the German national anthem for the wedding march when some church ladies rang the doorbell to pay a call. Everybody made it upstairs to hide except Simpson, who had to duck into the fireplace, and the hostess, who sat down with the ladies in the living room hoping they wouldn't notice the empty beer cans that had been used to construct an altar. Finally, when Simpson could no longer breathe, he stepped out of the fireplace and asked if he could fetch anybody a drink. Needless to say, the whole thing was highly entertaining when it happened, but we have at least as much fun telling about it, which we do all the time.

Simpson is useful to have around because he plays the piano and music is a key element in this business of keeping yourself entertained. Cobb's book contains an anecdote about an early flood, during which one Delta matron had scaffolding built for the grand piano so that her aunt Mamie could keep right on playing for the "overflow" parties. Boredom, after all, is not all we have to keep at bay down here—there are also the elements, and we like to be prepared for them. In 1990, for example, a man named Brown had predicted that a major earthquake would hit Memphis during the holiday season. Since Memphis, or more precisely, the lobby of the Peabody Hotel, is where the Delta is famously said to begin, an earthquake would have been bad news for my hometown, but by Christmas night everybody had pretty much decided to just forget about it. I was at my friend Jessica's house and her whole family is extremely musical so they were playing and singing, and the rest of us were dancing and drinking, and then at about three-thirty, we realized we had run out of whiskey. Fortunately, in preparation for the impending disaster, Jessica's father, Howard, had buried a few dozen half-pints of Canadian Club (his personal favorite) and assorted other booze in the backyard. So we went out and dug them up and were able to keep carrying on until dawn. Now, every time I see Howard, he puts his arm around me and says, "Baby, remember that time we got into my earthquake stash?"

But you don't have to have actually been there to enjoy a story. My father tells one about something that happened in the fifties that is way too long and too full of unexplainable nuances to repeat. Long before he gets to the punch line, he's laughing so hard he's crying and throwing his napkin in his face and being even more unintelligible than usual, but we all know every line by now, so we're all laughing too. This is often followed by a story he and his business partner try to tell that begins, "Remember that time we were sitting on that combine in Holly Bluff?" And that's it. That's all any of us have ever heard because they become so convulsed they cannot speak, but it makes me laugh like crazy just to think of them laughing. These are useful images to be able to call up because, let's face it, most days, on their own, are just not that funny.

Not long ago a friend of mine from London asked my father to tell him about the South, or at least the little piece of it where he lives. "What's it like there?" she asked. "Are there lots of brooks and streams?" Even when he's not telling a story he has a hard time keeping a straight face and this almost did him in. "Naw," he said, "but we got a lot of grudge ditches." Undeterred by a landscape marked primarily by grudge—otherwise known as dredge—ditches, she plans to visit anyway. He had tried to tell her one of his stories, and even though she had no idea what it was about, I think she wanted to experience one in the making.

The Morning After

Several years ago, I temporarily lost my mind and held a seated black-tie New Year's Eve dinner for thirty-two people at my house in New Orleans. It was complicated. I did all the cooking and setting up myself so I was exhausted by the time the party began. The four tables were on two floors and I had all the men change seats at the end of the second course, so the seating chart made my brain ache. When I woke up, hung over, the next day, I vowed never to do something so ridiculous again. I had no idea what a swell party it had been.

After many, many phone calls and face-to-face reports that filled my increasingly festive New Year's Day, I found out that: one female guest fainted after hearing another's detailed description of her recent tummy tuck surgery (I knew that she had fainted, of course, but I hadn't known why); one male guest introduced himself to the date of a friend of mine with the words, "So Julia tells me you're an arms dealer" (he was, but when I gave the speaker that titillating piece of information—years earlier—I hadn't expected him to repeat it to the man himself); my friend McGee was so insulted by something her first dinner partner said to her that she flipped him the universal gesture of disdain and turned her back on him until it was his turn to get up; and one male guest made such a lewd comment to another male guest that he simply walked down the stairs and out the door, never to return. It was so bad, apparently, that McGee's sister Elizabeth told me later that she thought I should print up pamphlets called "Appropriate Dinner Party Conversation" and leave them lying around the place.

But there was more: reports of who was doing what and with whom in the busy guest bathroom, and, most satisfactorily, a sighting of the former and occasional future love-of-my-life sitting on my bed holding his head in his hands. (He'd been tortured by his dinner partner, a close friend of mine who'd prattled on endlessly—and on purpose—about the virtues of Pablo Neruda, whose poems had formed the basis for an elaborate communications code during our affair.) Finally, there was a fistfight at my gate between two departing guests and my neighbors (who moved out shortly thereafter) and, last but not least, a visit from the fire department. I knew we'd been setting off (illegal) fireworks in my courtyard, but I didn't know, until the pictures came back, that what had set off the fire alarm had been the igniting of Roman candles in my bedroom.

It was a lot for one night and I had missed pretty much all of it. Hosts and hostesses almost always do. Which is why I am a great proponent of the after-party. The flowers are still fresh, the food is still good, there's usually some whiskey left, and the hostess can finally relax. More important, she'll be regaled about all the things she missed. My tutor in the art of the after-party is Anne Ross McGee, my mother's best friend, and mother of my friends McGee and Elizabeth. After Elizabeth's wedding, at which more than one thousand people had been present, Anne Ross woke me up, tossed me two painkillers and a muumuu, and told me to get to work, as she had invited 150 people over for lunch, which was coming up shortly. My first job was to clean up the garden, which is an ideal way for a hostess to learn about some of the more interesting goings-on at her party. On this particular morning, the debris on the lawn was innocent enough—bits of broken champagne flutes, lipstick-smudged cigarette butts, hundreds of wadded-up cocktail napkins. But then I ventured into the boxwoods, where more tantalizing items awaited. There was a single satin sling-back (that particular guest must have made an interesting exit) beneath one bit of shrubbery and an evening bag beneath another. The owner of the latter was so used to leaving it behind that there was a note pinned inside that began, "If found, please call . . ."

Anne Ross had not known that any specific comingling had occurred, she just figured from long experience that some probably had. After all, I myself had done some serious kissing on the roof of her house during her annual Christmas Eve buffet one year, and both of my shoes had been located next to an empty silver julep cup underneath a magnolia tree in the side yard after a particularly riotous summer shindig. The next morning, of course, I denied ever having seen them before. Thank God it hadn't been a piece of jewelry.

The most amusing (to me) denial I've ever had to give was to a host who had been really in the dark about the goings-on in his own house—because he hadn't been there. I am speaking of my father, who went with my mother and their friends to Mexico every New Year's Eve during the years I attended boarding school. Naturally, I took this opportunity to have an enormous annual New Year's Eve party in their house. One year, the party had somehow been announced from the bandstand at the local bar, and pretty much everybody in town (or at least all the members of what my mother might describe as "a certain element" and my father refers to simply as "riff-raff") showed up. Cars were parked all over the front lawn; our long-suffering maid was barricaded in my parents' bedroom with a .22. At one point during the evening, one wobbly guest backed into a table whose top consisted of a nineteenth-century Chinese porcelain platter. I considered it a miracle nothing far worse had happened, glued the table back together with Superglue, plied the maid with perfume, a gold necklace, and cash, and caught the plane back to Virginia. I was home-free, until years later, when the party's absentee host set his drink on the cracked porcelain tabletop and recoiled in indignation. "What the hell happened to this table?" he asked me. At first, of course, I instinctively insisted that I had no idea. But by this time I was about twenty-five years old, so I decided to go on and tell him. It would be amusing, I thought—it was not. Even though eight years had passed, neither he nor my mother greeted the tale with the delight a host or hostess usually takes in finding out what really happened at his or her party.

That party was fraught with danger. (The house could have burned down or the police could've come, the maid could've shot the couple who blundered into her bedroom hideaway, I could've been caught and taken out of school or worse.) But I have always said that danger—or at least the possibility of it—is a crucial element of any good party. Parties thrive on secrets that are made or told, alliances formed, dalliances done, someone striking a match in someone else's inappropriate heart. Once I was at an especially dangerous party where someone struck a match to the hostess's hair. And even then she was in the dark about it. What happened was this: The hostess was the sister of a much-beloved man, and among the guests was his less-beloved widow. As both women more or less hated each other's guts, there had been words early in the evening, but everybody, including the two women, forgot about them. Then the widow, sitting on the floor beside the coffee table, lit her cigarette using a lovely antique crystal match striker. The flame accidentally ignited the heavily teased and sprayed hair of the hostess, who was seated with her back to her sister-in-law. Since at first it was all that hair spray burning off, the hostess had no idea whatsoever that she was on fire—so her sister-in-law began beating on her head to put her out. The victim naturally assumed she was being assaulted by her enemy and turned around and punched her. By the time the two were separated, we had all decided that it was one of the best parties ever (and it bore out my theory that the combination of whiskey and fire generally enhances a party). The food had been really good, the music was great, but the fight made it. And the memory of it still entertains us to this day.

Snake World

When Hurricane Ivan tore into the United States Gulf Coast in September 2004, a lot of really terrible things happened, not least of which was the near decimation of the Florabama, the much beloved beach bar and package store that has straddled the Florida/Alabama line for more than forty years. The owners immediately vowed to rebuild, which was good news to most of the bar's regular musicians, who might otherwise have a hard time finding employment (with the notable exception of Larry T. Wilson, whose "The Only One for You Is the One and Lonely Me" should, in a perfect world, be a top-forty hit), and to former Oakland Raiders and New Orleans Saints quarterback Kenny Stabler, who leads the weekend-long interstate mullet toss every April (throwers line up with dead mullets—a trash fish disdained by most fisherman as well as diners—and toss them from Alabama to Florida, all in the name of charity). It also meant that I'd be able to spend another happy Easter on the Florabama's lower deck watching a man in a white bunny suit jump out of an airplane onto the beach. He hands out plastic eggs to children waiting with paper bags while their parents sit inside knocking back Bushwhackers, a powerful blend of Kahlúa, 151-proof rum, Coco Lopez, crème de Cacao, and ice cream that is among the bar's most popular drinks.

With all these activities, it is no wonder that Pubcrawler .com refers to the Florabama as "the greatest beach bar in North America" or that the bar's own website calls it "the last great American roadhouse." The Florabama is more than a bar, it's an institution, the Ground Zero of the Redneck Riviera, where it is possible to buy everything from lottery tickets (in the adjoining package store) to ankle bracelets to raw oysters on the half shell. A pilot who surveyed Ivan's damage immediately after the storm told *The New York Times* that the only thing that was keeping him from declaring the loss of the Florabama a true "cultural disaster" was the sure knowledge that it would rise again. Indeed, on the website there are constant photographic updates of its reconstruction, along with a message thanking its countless supporters for "keeping us in your thoughts."

As serious as the Florabama scare was, it was not nearly as unsettling as the news that another of Ivan's casualties was the Alabama Gulf Coast Zoo in Gulf Shores, home of a fourteen-foot, thousand-pound alligator named Chuckie, who was granted his freedom when the hurricane flooded his pond. It took five days to find him, during which many dire warnings were broadcast, including one from the zoo's general manager, Kate Ramon. "If you're a male, say six foot five, and he wants you, you're his," she told CNN, adding that since he was accustomed to regular feedings he was probably getting pretty hungry. Finally, the Alligator Retrieval Team from Orlando's Gatorland was brought in and they quickly spotted Chuckie in a ditch. After they secured him with a roll of duct tape (naturally), it took more than twenty-five law enforcement officers to pull him out and send him home. His capture was a relief, of course, but I was never all that bothered by Chuckie, on the theory that I would likely notice a half-ton alligator coming at me in enough time to get out of the way. What bothered me was the snakes.

The snakes, eight Burmese pythons, an anaconda, and twelve Colombian red-tailed boas, were all housed in the same zoo as Chuckie. Before Ivan made landfall, my friend Thomas Crampton wrote a piece in *The New York Times* about the zoo's hurried evacuation ("Noah Wouldn't Have Left Behind the Emus and Pythons"), and mentioned that the snakes, along with Chuckie, some waterfowl, and three emus, would all be fending for themselves during the storm. In Ivan's aftermath there were more pressing stories to report of death and devastation—not to mention the dramatic saga of the search for Chuckie—so the status of the snakes was never updated.

Now I am not an overly skittish person, but I really, really don't like snakes, and the prospect of several deadly ones crawling around anywhere near my neck of the woods made me nervous. I went out and bought the Smithsonian's book on snakes so I'd know what to expect just in case, and the news was not good, particularly with respect to the Burmese pythons. Their natural habitat is in rain forests and along riverbanks, which means that they'd be crazy about New Orleans, with its rain-forest-level humidity and convenient location along the Mississippi. The pythons are also "adaptable" enough to invade inner cities (we have one of those too) and riverfront warehouse districts (ditto), where they are attracted by the abundant rats. They are excellent climbers and swimmers, are active both day and night, and though they prefer to eat cats, dogs, and mongooses, at least one was seen swallowing a fifty-five-pound pig that was being prepared for butchering, and another was reported to have "grabbed, constricted, and swallowed" a fourteen-year-old Malay boy. At the end of this horrifying entry, it was noted that "nevertheless some snake hobbyists with small children allow pythons to roam freely about their homes."

This term "snake hobbyist" is not one that I can easily wrap my mind around, but there a lot of them out there apparently—so many that when my friend the novelist and *Wall Street Journal* Page One editor, Ken Wells, was growing up, he and his daddy and his six brothers made a good living in what he calls the "snake procurement business." They lived on Bayou Black near Houma, deep in south Louisiana's Cajun country, and worked for a character known as Alligator Annie, a neighbor who ran a reptile import-export business out of her house. (On Wells's website there is a memorable photo of his old boss draped with hundreds of black snakes.) Annie, who demanded live snakes only, paid ten cents apiece for garter snakes and green snakes, and fifty cents a pound for king snakes, chicken snakes, and nonpoisonous water snakes. For cottonmouths, copperheads, and rattlesnakes, she paid a premium, negotiated just before time of capture.

Wells says that in five or six springs and summers of snake hunting they all got "diabolically" good at it. On one memorable May morning, for example, they caught 120 garter snakes in an hour and sometimes the bag got so heavy it took two boys to carry it. They caught the garter snakes and pretty much everything else but the really bad guys with their hands covered in nothing but cheap gardening gloves. The venomous snakes, as well as the diamond-back water snake (a critter Wells describes as "unusually large and vicious, with the bite and disposition of a pit bull"), were caught using a long-handled contraption his father designed and had made at the sugar mill where he worked his day job.

I'm astounded by the bravery of the Wells boys, particularly during an especially harrowing face-off with a blue runner snake, which is, Wells tells me, "as fast as a scalded dog" and possessed of a "nasty temper, especially when you mess with it." To catch blue runners (called coachwhips in most other places), it is necessary to flush them out into the open and run them down. One day his father managed to get one out in a big cow pasture, and when it appeared to be getting away, he dove for it "much like a shortstop diving for a line drive." Unfortunately, he caught it too low and the thing whirled around and bit him right between the eyes. The boys had to pry it off, and for about a week, poor Mr. Wells walked around with a perfect impression of blue runner chops on the bridge of his nose.

Wells's point that there was good money in snake catching because there were "literally millions" of snakes where he lived makes me feel a tad ridiculous about being frightened of a handful of boas and pythons more than a couple of hundred miles away. I too grew up around millions (or at least many thousands) of snakes in the Mississippi Delta. I still carry around a news brief from my hometown paper about a guy who flipped his wrecker just east of Rosedale and was thrown into a ditch of poisonous snakes that bit him nine times. I got married not all that far from that spot and nothing that bad happened, although it could have. When the pictures came back of the pre-nuptial lunch—held at the lovely house of close friends—I noted the presence of an enormous snake coiled just outside the French doors to the terrace where we were all obliviously munching away on fried chicken and sipping Bloody Marys.

I might have been a little braver in the presence of snakes had I, like my buddy Wells, been paid to hunt them. Still, during my own first encounter with a snake, I have to say that I demonstrated more valor than my mother did. I was, I think, about four, and swimming with her in our brand-new pool. At the time, there was a guy who worked in our yard in whose intelligence she did not have a whole lot of faith. So when he told her that he couldn't come any closer to us because there was a rattlesnake in front of him, she didn't believe him for a second and insisted that what he was looking at had to be a limb that had fallen during the rainstorm the night before. That's when we heard its rattle, whereupon my mother instructed me to get out of the pool and run—right past the snake—into the house to tell Coatee what was happening.

Coatee Jones was the bravest woman I ever knew, even braver than the Wells boys. She had watched her mother get swallowed up by a tornado when she was ten, was married at thirteen, and lived in a tent on top of the levee after the 1927 flood destroyed the house on the land she worked as a sharecropper. Not a lot fazed Tee, so when I told her there was a rattlesnake in the yard, she was mostly irritated at the interruption to whatever it was she'd been doing. She stomped out to the toolshed, got a hoe, and then stomped over to the snake and dispatched it with one swift chop, after which she flipped it over on the hoe's handle and tossed it in the bushes, still writhing. I found the whole thing breathtaking, but for the rest of the day Tee went about her work disgustedly muttering and shaking her head over the general pitifulness and ineptness of white people.

I hate to think of all the water moccasins that must have been crawling around that levee where Tee camped after the flood, and of the many white people with dispositions like snakes whom she must have encountered in her time. The worst thing my mother ever says about anybody is that he or she is "mean as a snake." (Reptiles do not fare well in our house—her other favorite put-down is "crazy as a road lizard.") I don't think being compared to a snake is ever a good thing, unless perhaps you are a professional football player. Kenny Stabler's nickname happens to be "The Snake"—his website is called Snakesplace.com and its logo is an extremely menacing-looking cobra head. I am not sure if the name stems from his legendary ability to snake his way down the field or from the fact that when he played for the Oakland Raiders the team was known as the most unsportsmanlike in the NFL. Thank God they are resurrecting the Florabama. At the next mullet toss, I plan to turn up and ask him.

Color Me Red

About twenty years ago I attended the small afternoon ceremony that united in holy matrimony the waitress at my favorite local tavern and a guy named Dane, who was, I believe, an electrician. My date was my good friend Gus, who was the bartender at the same place and who was not real crazy about Dane because whenever he helped out at the bar he stole everybody's tips. Gus also claimed that Dane's eyes fluttered whenever he lied, which meant, therefore, that "his eyes are fluttering all the damn time." Anyway, there were about thirty of us seated on folding metal chairs at the local community center, and the pianist started playing the wedding march—Chicago's "Color My World"—but the groom hadn't taken his place next to the preacher and we could see the bride looking for him out the back door. The song was played four or five more times and everybody was getting nervous except for Gus, who was just disgusted, and then finally the groom showed up and the ceremony was performed. Over sandwiches and punch, which one of the groom's buddies had thoughtfully spiked, it emerged that Dane had been late because he'd been watching a stock-car race on TV and he hadn't been able to tear himself away until it was over.

I had not thought of that day in years, but I thought about it a lot during the 2004 presidential election, when NASCAR Dads replaced Soccer Moms as the voting bloc both candidates were so eager to attract and John Kerry was widely quoted as saying, "Who among us doesn't like NASCAR?" It turns out he didn't actually say it—he said something slightly less stilted—but *The New York Times*'s Maureen Dowd put it in her column and it was repeated four more times in the newspaper of record alone. By the time election night rolled around, *Newsweek*'s Howard Fineman cited the line on live TV as an example of why Kerry had lost the race—and embellished it further by replacing the word "among" with the even more damning "amongst."

Poor Kerry. The problem was that it *sounded* so much like something he would have said, no one ever bothered to check it. He'd already posed for *Vogue* carrying his windsurfing board (but not before dipping his head in the water and slicking his hair back for the camera), and he earned the derision of cheeseheads everywhere by calling Lambeau Field, the Green Bay Packers' home stadium, Lambert Field. Worse, after the Red Sox won the World Series, he bungled the names of two of his own home team's star players. I don't think he ever did go to a NASCAR event—he was misquoted at a union rally, not on a racetrack—and he was not invited to Charlotte, North Carolina, for the first ever NRA rally at a NASCAR race, which was attended by Senate majority leader Bill Frist and then Georgia senator Zell Miller and featured banners proclaiming NASCAR NATION IS NRA NATION and NASCAR FANS AND NRA FANS LOVE FREEDOM.

Now, I happen to like Kerry, and he can be good company—I had dinner with him once in Seattle and we talked for hours about the excitement of the running of the bulls in Pamplona (a dangerous event in which he once participated) and the nuances of the bullfights in Madrid—but I would not have begun to try to explain the goings-on at the aforementioned nuptials. Chief among the many things I doubt the good senator would have understood is that everybody accepted the groom's excuse for being late as perfectly valid, closely followed by the fact that "Color My World" is still overwhelmingly popular as a wedding march, and the detail that Dane wore a rented tuxedo even though it was three o'clock in the afternoon.

When I called Gus to check my recollection of the happy event, I told him I was reminded of it because of all the talk about NASCAR Dads. He said he didn't know if Dane had ever actually become a father, but that he remained "pretty representative" of a whole bunch of people in our part of the world. I think I can say with complete certainty that Dane is not representative of anyone John Kerry knows. On the trail, his discomfort with the big chunk of the electorate that used to be referred to as "good ole boys"—gun-toting, beer-drinking guys who are very clear about the difference between Lambert and Lambeau Field and who wept openly when Dale Earnhardt died—was palpable. Further, he didn't even try to make friends with anyone in the region where the term originated.

It wasn't really Kerry's fault—his party, as usual, decided to write off the South. This was a mistake because it appears that "good ole boy" culture is no longer confined to peanut farms and gas stations in rural Georgia. In 1976 Billy Carter was the president-elect's embarrassing redneck brother. These days he'd be a composite of a red state voter.

I may be exaggerating just a tad, and I don't think that any amount of campaign stops in Southern states would have helped Kerry, in particular, win the region, but he might have picked up a few tips that would've helped him in red states where the race was closer. Also, his almost complete avoidance of the place hurt our feelings—we are still very sensitive about Yankee condescension. As Zell Miller told a Fox News commentator, "Kerry never cared enough to come to the South to learn more about the people of the South, to learn more about the culture." Of course, Kerry could well have been scared off by Miller himself. With his nineteenth-century hairdo and menacing scowl, Miller is slightly reminiscent of the man I think of as our first redneck president, Andrew Jackson. Old Hickory was a big fan of dueling—he was known to get into gunfights on simple trips into town to pick up the mail—and during the Republican convention, Miller told MSNBC's Chris Matthews on live TV that he wished the practice were still legal so he could challenge him to one. Instead, he made do with a ferocious "Get out of my face!"

Still, Miller has a point. Had Kerry poked around a bit, he might have learned that long before anybody had heard of a NASCAR Dad, stock-car racing and politics were deeply intertwined. During the 1991 Louisiana governor's race between David Duke and Edwin Edwards, for example, I drove four hours to the small, mostly white town of Bunkie to witness Duke Night at the stock-car races, but alas, it was canceled. A year after the United States sent troops to Grenada, Speedway Motorsports CEO Humpy Wheeler reenacted the invasion at the Coca-Cola 600 in Charlotte, using helicopters, tanks, and more than six thousand "soldiers." Included in the action was the heroic rescue of Lug Nut, the track's mascot, from enemy forces and a trapeze artist who performed while hanging from a chopper.

That's another thing. Had Kerry ventured on down, he would have found out that we *liked* the invasion of Grenada. Most folks even like the invasion of Iraq. That's because we like to fight. Jackson, in addition to dispatching his own personal enemies, slaughtered hundreds of thousands of Native Americans on our home turf, and he remains extremely popular. Nathan Bedford Forrest was said to have sliced his adversaries in half with his sword while hollering and grinning. Not a lot has changed. At the NRA-NASCAR rally, a woman wearing a T-shirt with the likeness of Dale Earnhart on the front told a reporter that gun rights were an important issue for her because "we appreciate the right to defend ourselves if we have to."

Almost half of today's all-volunteer army comes from the rural South. There is no way of knowing if people enlist because of economic circumstances or patriotic fervor or both, but the region's patriotic sentiments can be easily measured by listening to country music stations. (Not surprisingly, there are far more of them in red states. Tennessee, for example, has ninety-seven to Massachusetts's eleven; Kentucky has ninety to Connecticut's five.) Long after even Dick Cheney gave up trying to make the connection between Osama bin Laden and Saddam Hussein, you could hear Darryl Worley allude to it almost hourly in his song "Have You Forgotten?" Then there is Toby Keith's hugely popular "Courtesy of the Red, White, and Blue," which includes the warnings, "This big dog will fight when you rattle his cage" and "We'll put a boot in your ass, it's the American way."

It must be said that it's not only the pickup truck-driving Danes of the world who agree with Toby Keith. Just before the election I was in Baton Rouge for a book festival, and I noticed a Volkswagen Jetta with a peace symbol on the rear window. Volkswagens and peace signs have long gone together, so I wasn't surprised to see one at a literary event even in Louisiana. But when I got closer I realized that the symbol was actually an outline of a B-52 bomber and the word "peace" was followed by the words "the old fashioned way."

This is why Howard Dean both missed the point and made a point when he professed his desire to be "the candidate for guys with Confederate flags on their pickup trucks." He is right that the Democrats should work harder at regaining a foothold in the South—and at understanding the red states, which now comprise much of the country—or they are doomed to be a minority party forever. He was just too tone-deaf to realize that the Confederate flag is not the smartest thing to embrace even in a throwaway line (after being hammered by everyone on both sides, he finally explained that he did indeed realize that the flag was a "loathsome" symbol). He was also too culturally isolated to realize that NASCAR Dads, or good ole boys, or whatever you want to call them, are not so easily stereotyped anymore; that they could well be driving a German-made car and attending poetry readings. Still, I think Dean would have been a more successful candidate in the South than the hopeless Kerry. For one thing, his famous exit speech after losing Iowa sounded an awful lot like an extended version of what we call a Rebel yell. Come to think of it, he looked a lot like Zell Miller in full throttle—or even Nathan Bedford Forrest in mid-slice.

Queen of the Turtle Derby

and Other Southern Phenomena

A Reader's Guide

JULIA REED

Questions for Discussion

1. In her introduction, Reed says that when she returned to her native South in 1991, there was a theory in vogue that the region was losing its identity as a separate place. She says she found plenty of proof that the South's identity is still firmly intact. Do her essays make a convincing case?

2. More than twenty years ago, John Egerton wrote *The Americanization of Dixie*. In the 2004 election, "NASCAR Dads" comprised a sought-after voting bloc and "red" states placed an emphasis on family and religious values that are typically seen as Southern. Also, every Southern state voted red. Do you think that it is now possible to make the case that it is the rest of America that is being Southernized?

3. On the basis of Reed's observations, would you say that politics and religion are more closely intertwined in the South than in other regions?

4. In "To Live and Die in Dixie," Reed quotes Mississippi writer Willie Morris, who said, "It's the juxtapositions that drive you crazy." She points out that Southerners are the most violent people in the nation but also the most religious. What are some other examples of double standards found throughout the book?

5. In "American Beauty" and "Southern Fashion Explained," Reed makes the case that women's looks are largely defined by their region. Do you believe that? If so, how would you describe the "look" of the place you live?

6. In "Miss Scarlett," Reed makes the case that Scarlett O'Hara was an early feminist. But she was also manipulative and used her beauty to get what she wanted. Have Southern women evolved from the Scarlett stereotype? In what ways do they still mimic Scarlett?

7. In one of the more memorable scenes from the film *Gone with the Wind*, Scarlett rips the silk curtains off the windows so that she can make a proper gown of them. On page 132 of "Miss Scarlett," Reed writes that Scarlett "was Southern, she was a woman, she was going to keep up appearances." Give

examples found in the book of the importance of "keeping up appearances" to both male and female Southerners.

8. Reed writes affectionately and enthusiastically about what she obviously feels is the superiority of Southern cuisine. Discuss the larger importance of food in Southern culture.

9. Throughout the book there are examples of well-meaning people who could easily be the objects of laughter or scorn— the beauty queen who supplies the title of the book, for example, or the man who swears he's grown closer to God since he found a cross-shaped sweet potato in his vegetable patch. Do you think Reed means to ridicule them, or does she succeed in painting an affectionate but clear-eyed portrait of the characters that populate her native land, despite their many foibles?

10. Reed gives several examples of Southerners' proclivity toward socializing, whether it be at a funeral or a party thrown the day after a party just because there was some whiskey left (page 177). What factors do you think contribute to the more aggressively social part of Southerners' natures?

11. Do you think that if Reed used the material in these essays to write a work of fiction, readers would have found it believable? Or are the stories included here a case of "truth is

stranger than fiction"? Give examples of some of the more outlandish—but true—tales found in the book.

12. Is there anything else about the South you wish you knew and would you prefer to learn it from fiction or nonfiction?

13. If you know the South well, do you think Reed has given an accurate portrait of its peculiarities? Why or why not?

PHOTO: © FRANCOIS HALARD

JULIA REED grew up in Greenville, Mississippi. She is contributing editor at *Vogue* and *Newsweek*. She also writes for *The New York Times,* among other publications. Reed lives in New Orleans.

About the Type

This book was set in Goudy, a typeface designed by Frederic William Goudy (1865–1947). Goudy began his career as a bookkeeper, but devoted the rest of his life to the pursuit of "recognized quality" in a printing type.

Goudy was produced in 1914 and was an instant bestseller for the foundry. It has generous curves and smooth, even color. It is regarded as one of Goudy's finest achievements.